GW00320184

Forza Italia

The Italian Triumph in the 2006 World Cup

Tony Limarzi

PublishAmerica
Baltimore

First printing

ISBN: 1-60474-607-6
PUBLISHED BY PUBLISHAMERICA, LLLP
www.publishamerica.com
Baltimore

Printed in the United States of America

In Loving Memory of
Leonor Sáenz Farías
December 28, 1914–September 26, 2004

For the love of the game

Acknowledgments

There's no way to thank all of the people who contributed to this book. Basically, if somebody's name appears on the following pages I wish to heartily thank them. There are some people who were very instrumental in this work, and they deserve special recognition.

I need to thank my three brothers: Pep, Mikey, and Johnny. Pep originally helped me get the format of the book in order. Mikey and Johnny were very hands-on with a lot of the editorial work. They both really enjoy telling me that I'm wrong, and they had a lot of chances to do so. My sister Nori was less involved with the specifics, but she provided needed support and was the most surprised and excited upon hearing the book was actually going to be published.

I owe everything to my parents. Mom always encouraged me to read a lot and enjoy books. I finally followed her advice. Pop instilled his passion and enthusiasm for Italian soccer in me, and without that, this venture would've been impossible. I also thank his father, Nonno, who did the same for him.

To my eldest child Lorenzo, we couldn't have done it without you. To my second son Luca, you have a beautiful name, and it's all thanks to the people in this book. Finally, I thank my wife for everything. All of the true joy and happiness in my life flows through her; nothing would have been possible without Meg.

1

A Team for the Ages

In American sports, you will hear the term "world" thrown around quite casually. Major League Baseball has a championship known as the World Series, but the best baseball teams in Japan are not included. The NBA crowns the world champions, but the world consists of more than just the geographical distance between the Miami Heat and the Los Angeles Lakers (even with the addition of the Toronto Raptors in 1995, world champions is a bit of a stretch).

Soccer's greatest tournament is known as the FIFA World Cup. The title of this competition is no overstatement. Every country has the right to compete, and every nation starts the tournament on equal footing. There are no politics involved. The country that wins enough games and proves itself superior to the competition earns the right to be called the best team on Earth.

The name "World Cup" applies to more than just the participating nations, but also to the people who will watch the tournament. One billion people watch the World Cup final match. That's one out of every six people on the planet. There is no other element of society in any culture on the globe that affects people in this way. There are many forms of entertainment which are common to all peoples in the world: music, movies, art. But it is impossible that one billion people would go to see the same movie, would buy the same album, or would attend the same exhibit in a museum. There is nothing that appeals to humankind like sports, and there is nothing in sports like the FIFA World Cup.

Every four years there is a FIFA World Cup champion, and each champion has a unique story of greatness. On rare occasions, the story of the World Cup champion is so incredible that it transcends sports and enters into the realm of true human greatness. Take the example of the 1986 World Cup champions, Argentina. The Argentine team was led by one of the greatest players in the history of the world, Diego Armando Maradona. Maradona was playing in his second World Cup, and after a disappointing tournament four years earlier, he was prepared to take his place as the greatest player on the planet. Over the course of that tournament in Mexico, Maradona did the impossible. At only five feet, six inches tall, Maradona took the rest of his team and the weight of his nation on his shoulders and carried them all to the World Cup championship. There has never been another World Cup winner that owed more to a single player; Maradona led his teammates in each match single-handedly (literally so against England). That tournament will always be considered *his* tournament, and even though there were teammates who complemented Diego's brilliance, it is 100 percent impossible that Argentina could have won without Maradona. Twenty years later, another World Cup champion has an equally enthralling story, but for the exact opposite reason.

After 24 years of failure in the FIFA World Cup, Italy reclaimed their spot on the throne of world soccer. In 1986 the glamour of the victory was the greatness of one man; in 2006 the beauty of the Italian triumph was the strength of the team. The Italian side was a collection of 23 players, but there were no individuals, just one team. The sports scene around the world at the time of the 2006 World Cup was filled with selfishness. Free agency was at an all-time high, unreasonable transfer fees meant that only the richest teams could afford the best players, and individual acclaim and recognition were more coveted than team accomplishments. It is because of these disheartening trends that the story of the Italian National Team is so unique and uplifting. The manner in which the players on this team fought so selflessly and tirelessly for each other temporarily restored a long-absent purity to the world's favorite game.

On rare occasions in sports, groups or individuals manage to break through the fan base of the specific sport and appeal to fans of sport in general. You don't have to be a hockey fan to recognize the accomplishments of the 1980 U.S. Olympic Hockey Team. You don't need to have ever seen a horse race to enjoy the remarkable life and career of Sea Biscuit. You don't need to be from the New England area to appreciate the unthinkable turnaround and long-awaited return to glory of the 2004 Boston Red Sox. And you don't need to be a soccer fan to be compelled by the 2006 Italian World Cup Championship Team.

Their story is based on many factors that represent the best values of humanity: teamwork, courage, overcoming adversity, responsibility, perseverance, and humility. Every Italian who hears the story of this team should be filled with pride. With the whole world watching, the Italian team put forth a perfect performance that can never be duplicated. As the years roll on and World Cup Champions come and go, the Italian team from 2006 will always remain as one of the greatest groups that put the true meaning back into the word "team."

2

Pep's Toast

As a rule, stereotypes are bad, and promoting them is worse. Individuals should be judged as individuals and not categorized by their appearance, background, religion, or country of origin. I want to make that very clear from the beginning, since most of the rest of this book will be unintentionally promoting a lot of stereotypes about Italians. In real life, I am not an Italian, I am an American. I was born and raised in the Washington, D.C., area. But, my father is a real Italian, born in Naples. He and his family actually moved to Brooklyn, New York, when he was very young. When I imagine my grandparents, aunts, and father moving to New York on the advice of one of their uncles to get rich quick by starting a shirt factory, I often envision scenes from movies I've seen with immigrants arriving in America. My family did so in the 1950s, and even though most of the movies I think of are set in the very early 1900s, I still envision my people climbing off the rat-infested ships that Hollywood loves to employ.

Soccer has been in my family for generations. Many years ago in the old country, my grandfather (or *Nonno* in Italian) was a professional referee. One famous story in my family lore is that in one specific game my grandfather awarded a late penalty kick to the visiting team, resulting in a home loss. The crowd went berserk, so much so that Nonno had to spend the night in the locker room to avoid the hostile locals. The next morning when he caught a taxi back home, the driver recognized him and asked him how in the world he could've possibly called that penalty. I am not 100 percent certain about the facts in the preceding story, but that is how the story is told by my relatives.

I grew up playing and watching soccer in suburban Washington, D.C. I was a pretty decent player through high school when I won a conference championship. In those days there was no professional league in the United States, so I never thought of soccer as a career, not that I was good enough anyway. In my youth, there really wasn't a U.S. national team either. The team may have existed, but they were not taken very seriously, which is why I became a staunch supporter of Team Italy. *Gli Azzurri*, which means "The Blues," have always been and will always be my favorite team, even with the fairly recent emergence of the United States. In the Olympics I always cheer for Team U.S.A., but world soccer is a different story. This is the one aspect of my life in which I am totally Italian.

Even though my competitive playing days ended in high school, I still managed to get a job in Major League Soccer, as the radio play-by-play announcer for D.C. United. This opportunity was my dream job. D.C. United was my home team from day one. I went to the games as a fan before I started working for the team, and once I got the job I never thought about doing anything else. The organization has been very good to me, and I have been totally blessed to be a part of the best franchise in the history of American professional soccer. I am very passionate about the team and about the game, and having the job I have, working for the team I love is an ideal situation. But, enough about me, let's get to the good stuff.

The following story, my story, is a lot like Hollywood, and at the same time nothing like Hollywood. My story is nonfiction, a true-to-life account of one wonderful year, highlighted by four amazing weeks. It does, however, have a cheesy ending, like so many popular movies. Like Hollywood, it promotes many stereotypes, as mentioned earlier. Don't forget: my story does not encourage the use of these stereotypes, it just happens to include a group of people who have characteristics that resemble the Italian stereotypes. Here are some such characteristics to look for. The Italians in my story are all a part of a large family. The Italians in my story love soccer. The Italians in my story are very passionate about life. The Italians in my story take eating very seriously. The Italians in my story enjoy yelling almost as much as they do eating. The patriarch of this Italian family has a moustache. Nearly all of the Italians in my story used to drive a Fiat (even though that has nothing to do with the story).

Before we move too far along, there are a number of reoccurring characters in this story, and I thought it might be better to give you a nice chart to refer to if needed. Here it comes:

Name	Nickname	Date of Birth	Relation to Author
Adolfo	Pop	11/29/1948	Father
Leonor	Mom	7/16/1949	Mother
Joseph	Pep	9/21/1974	Older brother (2 years)
Kristen	Kristen	10/27/1974	Sister-in-law (Pep's wife)
Tony	I or Me	10/30/1976	Self
Megan	Meg	3/17/1977	Wife
Leonor	Nori	7/30/1979	Younger sister (3 years)
Gioacchino	Gio	2/10/1977	Fiancé of sister
Michael	Mikey	8/11/1982	Younger brother (6 years)
Elizabeth	Liz	11/17/1983	Mikey's girlfriend
John	Johnny	1/1/1985	Younger brother (8 years)
Emily	Emily	12/12/1981	Johnny's girlfriend
Brigid	Brigid	2/8/2005	Niece
Alexander	Alex	2/8/2005	Nephew
Lorenzo	Lorenzo	8/14/2005	Son

Any individuals not included here will be introduced on a need-to-know basis.

* * * *

My story begins around Christmas of 2005. I was on the phone long-distance with Gio, in his hometown of Senise in Southern Italy.

We were talking about the upcoming World Cup tournament. As I had done for the previous five World Cups, I was commenting on the reasons why I thought Italy would be the World Cup champions. I don't know if I really believed what I was saying or if I was just saying it out of habit and hopefulness. I very clearly remember one thing that Gio said (he said it in Italian), "Really though, this is going to be a good year for Italy." I've talked with Gio hundreds of times, and I couldn't tell you anything we ever talked about, but for some reason this really stuck out to me. It's not like Gio is a sage. He loses money every week by betting on American sports. He still bets on the Lakers because of Magic Johnson. But when Gio made his comment about Italy in 2006, it seemed as though divine providence had entered our conversation. Suddenly Gio and I were on the same page, and even though I didn't have the heart to tell him that Walter Payton probably wouldn't make a big impact on the Bears game that weekend, I felt like Gio might have hit the nail on the head about the World Cup.

It was a special Christmas for my wife Meg and me. We had a wonderful four-month old son who was opening presents for the first time. Lorenzo didn't seem to understand exactly what was going on, but he liked to play with the paper, and he seemed to develop an immediate relationship with his new Cookie Monster puppet. Lorenzo also was generous enough to buy me a gift. I opened the shirt box and found a replica Team Italy jersey. The shirt was circa 1994 with the name and number of Roberto Baggio. That 1994 team was always a special one to me. Even though they lost in the final match, I always felt like that group of players led by one of the greatest ever had a truly magical tournament, and in many ways deserved to be world champions. I don't know how Lorenzo at barely four months old knew to get me the perfect gift, but that's just what it was. I think his mom must have helped him pick it out.

There were still six months to go before the first match of the 2006 FIFA World Cup, but it was one of the things that I was continually thinking about. I can't say that I lost any sleep over it that far in advance, but there were many nights that I would think about the upcoming tournament as I was falling to sleep. I also thought about the frustration of the previous World Cups. I had trouble deciding which one was the most disappointing. It seemed like each one's tragedy was unique. In 1990 Italy was defeated in a penalty shootout for the first time. That tournament was held in Italy, and the home defeat was probably the saddest. I remember being unable to watch the remaining matches; I felt like someone I loved had died. In 1994 the team lost again in a penalty shootout. In the olden days, the FIFA rules stated that if a World Cup final was still tied after overtime, then instead of penalties the game would be played again. The idea was that the final game is too important to be decided in a shootout. That idea changed, and Italy was defeated in Los Angeles. When I think back on that tournament I can still enjoy the positive memories from Baggio and company; I just sort of shrug about the final result. In 1998, Italy had a good team in which Baggio had an important reserve role. Christian Vieri emerged as a new Italian goal-scoring superstar, and there were a bunch of young players who could've been the perfect complement to the veteran leaders. That team's tournament run ended in a shootout in the quarterfinals. Once again the cruel injustice of the penalty shootout reared its ugly head to stop a team that probably deserved at least a shot in the semifinals. The World Cup in 2002 was an absolute disaster. Italy was mistreated by the refs who missed a number of clear calls that cost Italy two games, and they were eliminated in the round of 16 by an inferior South Korea squad. The worst news of all about that tournament was that it was played in Japan and Korea, so I had to watch all the matches in the middle of the night, and I was exhausted and cranky for four weeks straight. The best part about World Cup 2002 was that it eventually ended.

In celebration of the final game of that tournament, my family had a brunch to watch the final between Brazil and Germany. We had lots of good breakfast foods, complemented by mimosas. As Pep opened the champagne to mix with the orange juice he offered a toast. "I brought two bottles of champagne, one French bottle and one Italian bottle. The champagnes represent the last World Cup champion (France in 1998) and the next World Cup champion (Italy in 2006)." We all shared a laugh and thought, "I'll drink to that!" I don't know if Pep was serious or just trying to cheer us up, but at least once the 2002 World Cup was finally over, every nation on Earth was back on level terms in preparation for Germany 2006.

3

Four Years of Anticipation

June 30, 2002, was a significant date in world football. It was especially important for Brazil, since that was the day that they defeated Germany 2-0 to win their fifth World Cup championship. This date was important for the rest of the world not only because of the significance of Brazil's accomplishment, but also because it marked the unofficial beginning of the 2006 FIFA World Cup. Once Brazil lifted the trophy to bring an end to the tournament in Japan and Korea, every other nation was back in the hunt, vying for the next crown.

The quest for that crown is a grueling one. For every country except the host nation, the qualifying process is a remarkable journey. Qualification begins with 204 countries from all six continental regions, and is eventually whittled down to the 32 countries that will reach the World Cup finals. The entire process lasts for about two years, but with the amount of anxiety that comes with every game it feels more like 20.

Some of the continental zones are more forgiving than others. This is the way it was all decided for Germany 2006.

The qualifying system was the most straightforward in South America. There were ten teams in the region; each team played the other nine teams twice, once at home and once on the road. The top four teams in the standings after the 18 games advanced to Germany.

For Brazil and Argentina, the World Cup is almost a sure thing. Even if Brazil loses a game or two, and even if Argentina has a handful of ties, they're both almost assuredly going to finish in the top four. Barring a national catastrophe, these two superpowers will be in the World Cup for the next 160 years.

The African path to Germany was far less predictable. There were 51 nations competing from the continent, nine of whom received free passage into the second stage of their qualifying. The other 42 countries were randomly paired off to play a two-game series, home and away, where the team with the most goals after the two games advanced. The 21 winning nations joined the nine pre-qualified teams in the final stage of African qualifying. Those 30 teams were divided into five groups of six teams each. Every team played every other team twice (home and away), and the five group winners were on their way to Germany.

The key difference between Africa and South America (besides the number of World Cup champions the continents have) is that there are fewer opportunities to make up for mistakes in a 10-match league as opposed to an 18-match league. Plus, in order to go through from Africa, the countries have to be the best team of the group, not simply in the top 40 percent. This slim margin for error was part of the reason why the African favorites struggled during 2006 qualifying. As a result, four of the five African representatives were making their debut in Germany.

The CONCACAF region, which consists of North America, Central America, and the Caribbean, is consistently a top-heavy one. Mexico had always been the most formidable country, but the United States has pulled even over the past few years. This part of the world is basically a two-horse race, but the continental zone would send three teams to Germany.

Asia is another region in which the cream rises to the top rather quickly. South Korea and Japan always seem to have a relatively easy time making it to the final stage, and they were both rejuvenated by their co-hosting excitement from the last World Cup.

The European qualifying process was more elaborate. The teams were ranked and divided into eight groups. Every team played every other team in their group twice and the eight group winners moved on to Germany. Furthermore, the two best second-place teams out of the eight groups also advanced to Germany, while the remaining six second-place teams advanced into a playoff. These six teams were randomly drawn into three pairs that played a two-game playoff. At last, the three winners of these final series made their travel arrangements to Germany.

There was also one final set of playoffs to round out the field of 32. Four other nations got one last chance to advance to the World Cup through an amazing inter-continental playoff. FIFA couldn't really decide if Asia or CONCACAF deserved an additional entry to the tournament, so they decided to let them go nose-to-nose to decide for themselves. The fourth-place team from CONCACAF played a two-game series versus the fifth-place team from Asia: winner take all. A similar two-game playoff was played between the fifth-place team from South America and the top team from the Oceanian zone (Australia and the surrounding nations). These were the final two teams to make the tournament. These were teams number 31 and 32, the last two nations that would read "Wilkommen" at the airport when they landed in Germany.

The qualification process for the FIFA World Cup is the most intricate in all of sports, and it is difficult to thoroughly understand all of the specifics. Imagine having to play your way through it.

* * * *

Theseus was a Greek mythological leader who negotiated his way though the labyrinth, killed the Minotaur, and found his way back out to return home safely. His saga is not unlike World Cup qualifying. In fact, even Theseus' trip through the labyrinth was not filled with the number of twists and turns that every team goes through during qualification. Despite the reference, the Greeks did not qualify for Germany 2006.

Players get injured. Coaches get fired. The press maligns the team. Players retire. Coaches fight with the administration. The press maligns the coach. Players come out of retirement. Coaches resign. The press criticizes the coach for resigning. And that's just the first half of the journey. There are always a few shocking results, but as the process crawls towards the finish line, there are many more expected protagonists than unexpected ones.

* * * *

By the fall of 2005, most of the field of 32 was already set. Germany had been waiting for three years to see who would officially be joining them. Brazil and Argentina finished at the top of South America (yawn!), followed by Ecuador and Paraguay. Japan, South Korea, Saudi Arabia, and Iran advanced from Asia. North and Central America sent U.S.A., Mexico, and Costa Rica, just like four years earlier. For Africa, only Tunisia had made it this far before, as Cote d'Ivoire, Ghana, Angola, and Togo were all ready to set sail on their maiden voyage in the World Cup finals. In Europe, Holland, Ukraine, Portugal, France, Italy, England, Poland, Serbia and Montenegro, Croatia, and Sweden were in.

At this point, 27 of the 32 teams were set. The remaining five teams would be decided by the home and home playoff series. In Europe, Spain used a 5-1 rout against Slovakia to clinch a spot in Germany, while the methodical Czech Republic advanced behind a pair of 1-0 wins over Norway. Switzerland withstood a frantic finish from Turkey to finalize their travel itinerary and to close the book on European qualifying.

The only teams left would emerge from the inter-continental playoffs. Australia beat Uruguay by winning a penalty shootout in front of nearly 83,000 supporters in Sydney. The Socceroos had qualified for the first time since World Cup 1974 in West Germany. A world away, there was an enormous battle from one of the smallest countries. The tiny island nation of Trinidad & Tobago defeated the Asian country of Bahrain to advance to their first World Cup finals ever.

At last, the field was set—32 countries to be divided into eight groups of four teams each. Once the teams were known, the experts started to predict the next champion. Naturally, Brazil was the clear favorite. The samba dancing magicians had already won the tournament five times including 2002. The defending champions had the same core group of players plus a few outstanding newcomers, all working around Ronaldinho, regarded as the best in the world. For most people, the real discussion should be about who Brazil's opponent would be in the final.

Some more courageous prognosticators sided with France. The French team was getting older, but this would be the final World Cup for their inspirational leader Zinedine Zidane, and his greatness would be enough to carry the team through. Argentina was a popular choice among soothsayers. They were a talented group of youthful but experienced players, including perhaps the best young player on the planet in Lionel Messi. They finished tied with Brazil during the South American qualifying—what more needed to be said?

There were some sentimentalists who thought that Germany could win the tournament on their home turf. Juergen Klinsmann, one of the greatest players in the nation's history, was now running the team as the head coach, and it would certainly be a wonderful storybook ending to the tournament. England was considered to have a legitimate shot at bringing home their second World Cup title. They had talent, consistency, goal-scoring ability, and a tough-nosed defense. Finally, there were the rumblings of, "Maybe this will finally be their year," a phrase that could have been applied to Holland, Spain, or Portugal.

There was no talk whatsoever about the Italians. Italy was a three-time World Cup champion, but they hadn't won a championship since 1982. Nobody thought very much of them; some even went so far as to say they weren't a world power of soccer anymore. They play too defensive, and they don't score enough. In a world of the dramatic attacking flair of Brazil, Argentina, and Portugal, the boring style of the Italians didn't stand a chance. And besides all of the tactical reasons why they couldn't get past the quarterfinals, there was a scandal of corruption in their domestic league. The Italians had enough to worry about on their own without throwing Brazil or Germany into the mix. No, the Italians just didn't have the firepower for this World Cup; maybe if they got everything in order back home they'd have a chance in 2010.

4

Fabio Who?

Team Italy is not one of America's favorite teams; I think it comes from their partnership with the Germans in World War II. During World Cup qualifying, pretty much any England or Ireland match can be found at a local pub or soccer bar. To watch Italy, you have to really search out a lot of pizzerias to find one that has a satellite dish with RAI International. RAI is the national public broadcasting company of Italy, and there is an international channel which shows Italian programming all of the time. If the Italian national team is playing, people around the world can usually find the game on RAI International.

A few World Cups ago, Pop decided to get a satellite dish (after getting tired of having to go to Three Brother's Pizzeria in Greenbelt, Maryland). He doesn't pay for any sports package or movie channels; he only uses the satellite for RAI International. That's the only channel you can see from the dish. You have the potential to watch over 1,000 channels, but Pop only wanted one, so that's all he pays for. My family always likes to watch significant matches together, and since the games are only on at Mom and Pop's house, that's where we normally gather.

The road to Germany for Team Italy was a relatively comfortable one. They won their first two matches, and then had a startling loss to Slovenia, before winning two more in a row. It looked all along like they would qualify in first place and avoid the difficult European playoff.

The process was winding down for Group Five in September of 2005. On September 3, Italy was playing a match in Glasgow against Scotland. On this day I was traveling to Denver, Colorado, with my broadcasting colleagues Dave Johnson and John Harkes. We were in town for the D.C. United game that night, and before we had to be at the stadium, we all went to the ESPN Zone to see the World Cup qualifying.

We sat down to watch the game, which was much more important to Scotland since they needed to make a quick climb up the standings in order to sneak into the playoffs. John Harkes is of Scottish descent, so he was cheering for Scotland. Also, since he wasn't Italian, he pretty much rooted against Italy unless they were playing Germany, just like the rest of the world.

Many American soccer fans know John Harkes very well. He was a longtime captain of the U.S. men's national team, he was the original captain of D.C. United, he was a two-time MLS Cup champion, and he is a National Soccer Hall of Fame inductee. At this point, he was also the TV color analyst for the D.C. United games, which is why we were traveling together to Denver.

Well, much to John's delight, and my frustration, Scotland scored in the 16th minute to go ahead. John told us that his father, watching the match at the local Knights of Columbus meeting hall in Kearny, New Jersey, would be loving life. (Technically, I don't remember what specific men's club Mr. Harkes was with that day; it may not have been the Knights.)

Anyway, Scotland held onto their lead deep into the second half, when Italy scored (some guy that I had never heard of named Fabio Grosso). Italy was almost a lock to take first place in the group after the tie, and in some ways I felt bad for Mr. Harkes back in New Jersey, who must have had a sad trip home knowing that he'd have to watch the second consecutive World Cup without Scotland.

Both of my friends at lunch would move on to work at the World Cup in 2006. John was a TV analyst for the ESPN family of networks, and Dave Johnson, the regular D.C. United TV play-by-play announcer, called radio play-by-play for satellite radio during the tournament.

After that 1-1 tie, Italy won their last three matches and cruised into the World Cup. They managed to do so in convincing fashion, something which is highly unusual for the team that normally waits until the situation is absolutely dire before playing their best. For some reason, they didn't want to take any chances this time, and they gave their fans a few rare moments of relaxation. For me, any moment to relax during Italy matches is much appreciated.

The European World Cup qualifying came to an end a few weeks later, and the next significant event would occur when the final groups were decided. That ceremony is always intense, and it's the first time that fans around the world get their pencils and paper ready to start mapping out the road to the final. I didn't need pencil and paper; we had Mikey's laptop.

5

The Group of Life

On Friday, December 9, 2005, the world watched the unofficial opening ceremony of the 2006 FIFA World Cup. On this day, the 32 teams that had qualified for Germany were sorted into the eight groups that would shape the first stage of the World Cup finals. This dramatic spectacle was not unlike the Powerball lottery. In both drawings, the hopes and dreams of millions were riding on the outcome, the entire process would only last a few moments, and everything was determined by little plastic balls. The main difference was that the Powerball could only present the winner with a multimillion-dollar prize, whereas the World Cup lottery would be the foundation for eternal glory.

The 32 teams were divided into four bowls. The first team selected was placed in Group A, the next team in Group B, and so on through Group H. After each group had one team, the process was repeated A through H, until all groups were full with four teams. To give the event the glamour that it deserved, a group of celebrities was invited to take part in the selection. Each ball was selected by a celebrity (the most memorable being the lovely and talented Heidi Klum), and presented to the FIFA appointed judge. The judge then cracked it open to reveal a small piece of paper from inside (just like a fortune cookie). On the paper, there was the name of a team. Then another celebrity chose another ball which revealed the team's position within the group (one through four). Ultimately, all 32 teams would know their group, opponents, and match schedules.

The first of the four bowls contained the top eight teams in the tournament, as determined by a series of criteria which are slightly too confusing to address here. Those teams were Argentina, Brazil, England, France, Germany, Italy, Mexico and Spain. The remaining teams were placed into three bowls according to geography so that no two teams from the same continental zone could be placed in the same group (with the obvious exception of the many European teams). Each final group consisted of one team from each of these bowls.

This elaborate ceremony could provide the first bit of luck for the World Cup, which would begin exactly six months after selection day. The selection process was totally random within the parameters, but somehow each World Cup invariably has one group which is the most difficult: *The Group of Death*. There are good teams and bad teams in every bowl, and without fail, several good teams from the different bowls will end up in the same group. For Germany 2006, the Group of Death was Group E: Italy, Ghana, U.S.A., and Czech Republic.

The pundits dove head first into the Group of Death: Italy always makes it out of the group phase; Ghana is the "Brazil of Africa"; the U.S.A. was inches away from the semifinals four years earlier; the Czech Republic has one of the best players in the tournament in Pavel Nedved. Which two teams would advance from this group? Italy and Czech Republic? Italy and U.S.A.? Czech Republic and U.S.A.? Czech Republic and Ghana? Ghana and U.S.A.? There were still six months of anxious waiting to see which teams would emerge heroically from the Group of Death.

There was an even more important question than who would advance from this group, and that was who would finish first. The tournament was set up so that in the round of 16, the winner from Group E would play the runner-up from Group F, and vice-versa. Brazil would almost assuredly win Group F, so the best way to avoid Brazil was to win the Group of Death. Easier said than done. At any rate, there wasn't much hope for any of the teams in Group E to really threaten for the title. If you finish in fourth place or third place in the group, you get eliminated; if you finish in second place in the group, you lose in the round of 16 to Brazil; if you finish in first place in the group, you've spent all of your energy and good play in the first three games, and you've got nothing left in the tank. It seemed cut and dry to the analysts, but there was one thing that they failed to consider.

Confidence. Confidence is such a valuable commodity in a tournament environment. It is fragile and fickle. It comes and goes without explanation, but if a team can harness it and maintain it, confidence can be more important than any other single attribute. It seemed possible that if a team from Group E managed to make it through those three dangerous matches in first place, then that team could use the confidence gained from winning the toughest group in the tournament to propel themselves into the semifinals or farther. It would not be an easy task; in fact it would be *two* difficult tasks: first finishing at the top of the Group of Death, and second maintaining the confidence without letting it mutate into overconfidence. Accomplishing these two objectives would fall in large part onto the shoulders of the team's head coach.

Marcello Lippi was the head coach of the Italian national team. When the groups were finalized, he knew that Italy was a favorite to advance, but he also knew that all the teams in Group E were very dangerous. Ghana had beaten Italy 3-2 in the 1996 Olympics, and in that match the speed and athleticism of the Africans caused all sorts of problems for the usually solid Italian defense. Team U.S.A. scored three quick goals to open their World Cup in 2002. The Americans had improved in the last four years, and were still trying to erase the bad memories from four years earlier when they felt that the referee missed a clear hand ball on the goal line against Germany. Czech Republic beat Italy in the European Championships in 1996, and their best player, Pavel Nedved, played in Italy for Juventus, so he and his team would be well prepared for whatever tactics Lippi (Nedved's former coach) could draw up. Each team posed serious threats, and each team's weapons were unique. For Lippi, there was a great deal of research in preparing for the three teams that Italy would face, but as it is for many coaches, the key to success would be making sure his own team was at its best. There were many factors working against him in that regard.

The negative publicity at home for the Italians was intense. For a nation that is crazy for *il calcio*, the fact that many of the best Italian club teams were under investigation for influencing league referees was bigger news than the presidential election going on simultaneously. Lippi's former team, Juventus, was at the center of the scandal, and there were some who were calling for his resignation from the national team before the World Cup began. There were other problems as well.

Gianluigi Buffon, the national team's starting goalie, who also played for Juventus, was under investigation for betting on league matches. Besides these problems, Italy's most famous and creative player, Francesco Totti, was still recovering from a broken ankle, and it was unclear how much he would be able to help the team on the field.

In the weeks leading up to the World Cup, there were more doubts than ever: the Group of Death, a disastrous scandal back home, the distractions for the starting goalie, the ankle of the playmaker, and an incredibly critical press waiting to crucify anyone at the first key misstep. For Lippi, there was only one way to approach the task at hand: focus on the controllable aspects of his team. The scandal in Italy was in the hands of the investigating committee; Buffon's contributions would depend on his own mental focus; the team doctors were constantly monitoring Totti's ankle; and the Italian media was never going to change. What Lippi *could* do was to make sure that, in spite of the ominous distractions, his team was as prepared as possible both physically and mentally to earn a win in their first World Cup match against Ghana. Perhaps once the tournament finally got underway for the Italians, Germany could be a sanctuary for Lippi and his players.

6

Worst-Case Scenario

When we gathered together to watch the final group selection, we all pretty much agreed what we were hoping against. With all of the possibilities, there were some which would create a much harder group for Italy than others. For example, we knew that there would be one other European team in Italy's group. It could be someone very tough like Czech Republic or the Netherlands, or it could be someone easier like Switzerland or Poland. Similarly, the next bowl could present the likes of lowly Togo or Angola, or the dangerous side of Ghana. Also, there was the bowl that had Team U.S.A. in it. The United States was the toughest team in their bowl, but also, if they were placed into Italy's group, it would make it harder on my family for a number of reasons.

I have already expressed my allegiance to Team Italy. This was never really a decision for me, since I knew Italian soccer before there was American soccer. When it comes to sports, my family and I always agree. We've always been very close, and we've always supported the same teams. But somehow, when it comes to cheering for the U.S. soccer team, our family is divided. It seems like those families in the 1850s who had one brother fighting for the Confederates and another fighting for the Union. Our family lines were drawn. I was on the side of Team Italy, alongside Pop, and Nori. Pep, Mikey, and Johnny would support the United States above all others. For Mikey and Johnny, the response is understandable, since by the time they were aware of world soccer, the U.S.A. was a mainstay in the World Cup. For Pep, there is no excuse. He's older than me and should be an even stronger supporter of the family ties than I am. Sometimes he used to do things just to help out his much younger brothers; maybe he pretends to prefer Team U.S.A. for their sakes. As for Mom, she follows her own ancestry and quietly cheers for Mexico. At any rate, it wouldn't matter, since the odds were pretty long that Italy and U.S.A. would be in the same group. Chances were that U.S.A. and Italy would not go head to head, and we could all cheer for both teams with equal emotion. In conclusion, we knew the worst-case scenario would be a group with Italy, Czech Republic/the Netherlands, U.S.A., and Ghana; the best case would be Italy, Switzerland, Trinidad & Tobago, and Togo.

As the teams started to be announced, the worst-case scenario was unfolding before our eyes. When they cracked open the ball from the U.S.A. bowl to be placed in Italy's group somebody in the room said, "Please, anybody but U.S.A." The French-accented announcer on TV said, "United States." It would have been pretty funny if it hadn't been so upsetting. The exact worst-case scenario was now a reality. It didn't negatively affect the family dynamic yet, since there was still an outside chance that both Italy and U.S.A. would advance, but we were all pretty cranky. Mikey, who was not with us on that day, called and started yelling about how Mexico got to be the head of a group instead of us. By "us" he meant U.S.A.; if he had been a little less sad I probably would have egged him on by saying, "You mean, *you*, right, because *us* is Italy." I realized it wasn't the right time. There were still six months until the opening game, and it didn't make sense to get overanxious at this time.

On paper, Italy still had a pretty good chance of advancing, and a good chance of coming in first. Unfortunately, they rarely play the matches on paper; FIFA had already decided to use the fields in the fancy new stadiums in Germany. I did not want U.S.A. to fail. My ideal scenario would be for Italy to advance in first place and Team

U.S.A. to go through in second. However, Italy's progression was of the utmost importance. So then, if U.S.A. needed to lose for Italy to go through I would cheer against U.S.A., but hopefully they could both move on. A few months later, there was another wrinkle added to my Team U.S.A. equation. His name was Ben Olsen.

Ben Olsen was named to the final 23-man World Cup roster for the United States. Olsen was a veteran of D.C. United. He had played his entire career with D.C., and he was a local hero. During his career he had been named Rookie of the Year and MLS Cup MVP. He was always very friendly and approachable, which is not common in pro athletes. I respected Ben Olsen as much as any athlete in any sport. Once he was named to the roster, it seemed almost unfair for me to wish him anything less than the ultimate success, but I loved Team Italy before I loved D.C. United, and even though I *did* want him to have a great tournament, I didn't want it to happen at the expense of the Italians. I envisioned a match between Italy and U.S.A. ending with the Italians winning 3-2, with Olsen scoring both goals for the Americans.

As I noted earlier, I was the radio play-by-play announcer for D.C. United. I was also the backup TV play-by-play announcer for the local cable broadcasts of D.C. United matches. The regular announcer, Dave Johnson (he was with us in Denver, remember?) was going to miss a bunch of United games while he was working in Germany, so I was scheduled to work on the TV side for five D.C. United games during the season. The first one was on June 3 when D.C. United hosted New England. On that day, John Harkes was the analyst. United won 1-0. As we were wrapping up our broadcast I took a moment to tell the viewers that John would be leaving our D.C. United coverage to go work in Germany for the World Cup. I wished him well, told him to have fun, and asked him to make sure Team U.S.A. didn't beat Italy, maybe they could tie. We said goodnight to the viewers, and John was off to Germany.

* * * *

The tournament was set to begin on June 9, with the host nation Germany playing Costa Rica. June 9 is my wedding anniversary, and June 9, 2006, was my five-year anniversary. My gracious wife, who is as wonderful as she is beautiful, decided that we could go out to celebrate our anniversary one day early so that I wouldn't have to be distracted once the tournament began. We had a wonderful dinner together and talked about how much we missed Lorenzo (it was only the second or third time we'd used a baby-sitter) and how excited I was about the World Cup. At one point, Meg said something about how it would be great if Italy won. I told her that it was sweet of her to say so, but I didn't want to think about it; I was pretty anxious. Plus, like a wounded lover who had been burned too many times, I didn't want to get my hopes too high about Team Italy.

We continued to have a wonderful anniversary dinner with nice conversation. It was especially nice not to have to cut any food into tiny pieces or make sure applesauce didn't get thrown on the floor. We had started to talk about maybe having another child soon. Meg had always liked the name Luca, which was not very high on my list of favorites. She made a deal with me: "How about if Italy wins the World Cup, then we name our next son Luca?" I thought that if Italy was going to win the World Cup, then Luca Toni would need to be a hero; in which case, it would be worth it. Plus, I'd be willing to name our next child Beelzebub if it meant Italy winning the World Cup. "Okay, if Italy wins the World Cup, we'll name our next son Luca." I wanted to change the subject, since the talk of Italy winning the World Cup was a little too much. It felt like when you talk about winning the lottery and you already have plans on how to spend the money. Then it's surprisingly sad when you don't win the 265 million dollars. I didn't want to focus too much on the pie in the sky; I was more concerned with the pie on the dessert cart. We finished our dinner and raced home to be with Lorenzo.

Meg and I had dated since the early spring of 1994. This would be our fourth World Cup together and our first with Lorenzo. That night, I couldn't get to sleep with all the anticipation, so I watched Lorenzo sleep for a little while. Meg worked during the day, so Lorenzo and I would be watching all the games together, since they came on in the mid-afternoon. I was excited for his first World Cup, but I also looked forward to watching the games with my kid for the first time. Even though he didn't understand exactly what was going on at Christmas, we still celebrated it with him. And this tournament was even bigger than Christmas, since you get four Christmases for every one World Cup. Everybody always says that having a child changes your life in ways you can't imagine. I don't know how to explain it, but in the same way, I felt like now that we had Lorenzo, everything was going to be different.

* * * *

Finally the big day arrived. Monday, June 12 featured a triple header of World Cup matches, culminating with the main event for me: Italy vs. Ghana. In the first match, at 9 a.m. EDT, Australia used a frantic comeback to defeat Japan. I always forget how enjoyable it is to watch World Cup games when there is no personal stake in the outcome. I could admire the three quick goals from the Australians without worrying too much on the impact it might have on the Japanese fans. For the next two matches that day, I would not have the luxury of watching without emotional attachment. At noon, Team U.S.A. kicked off against Czech Republic in the opening match of the Group of Death. Death came quickly for the Americans. After only five minutes, the Czechs went ahead. Then they doubled their lead before halftime. Finally, they added the salt on the American wound for the 3-0 final. As the match was in the final stages, Pep said to me, "We waited four years for *this*?" Poor Pep was pretty sad.

I've made it quite clear that I cheer for Team Italy, but I want everyone to know that I am not anti-American. I was very sad with the outcome of the first match for the United States. I wanted Italy *and* U.S.A. to advance to the next round, and it looked like a long shot after the debacle of Czech Republic vs. U.S.A. But when Pep looked so upset about the American game I felt like saying, "Yeah, well at least it wasn't Italy that lost three to zero." I didn't say it for two reasons: first, I was upset by the result too; second, I didn't want to jinx the next match.

The long wait was at last coming to an end. After four years of having the taste of the loss to Korea in my mouth, Italy was about to start a new series of World Cup memories. Lorenzo and I were at my parents' house with Mom, Pop, Pep and his kids, Mikey, my aunt Maria, and one of Mikey's friends from graduate school, a Trinidadian named Sid. Mikey and Sid were both studying to get their PhDs in mathematics from Johns Hopkins University. I just hoped that $I > g$; where I represents the total number of goals for Italy and g represents the total number of goals for Ghana. The family room was filled with a lot of anxiety, especially after the disastrous result from just a few minutes earlier. No more formalities, it was time for the kickoff.

7

Match Day 1—June 12
Italy vs. Ghana—Hanover

On the fourth day of the FIFA World Cup, Italy was to take the field against Ghana. Germany, England, Argentina, Holland, and Portugal had all won their first matches. The other match from Group E had been played earlier that day, and Czech Republic defeated U.S.A. 3-0. The game was a powerful display by the Czechs; Italy needed a victory to keep pace. For Ghana, it was their first World Cup appearance ever, but if they allowed the enormity of the moment to get to them, they would surely have no chance to defeat Italy. Italy's team captain and central defender Fabio Cannavaro was a member of the Olympic team that lost to Ghana ten years earlier; it's difficult to say whether a win in this match could be considered revenge for that defeat.

The players finally made their way onto the field, heard their national hymn echoing through the stadium, shook hands with their opponents and the match was underway. Italy was dressed all in blue, living up to their national nickname *Gli Azzurri*. Italy came out with an aggressive start, as perhaps there were some opening nerves for Ghana. In the opening minutes Italy was forcing Ghana back to defend, and when Ghana managed to move forward on the attack, Italy struck back with quick counterattacks. Italy was the better team for the first half hour, but Ghana did push forward when they had the chance, and their defense kept Italy off the score sheet—barely. The best chance for Italy came from their talented striker Luca Toni.

Toni was coming off a spectacular season in Serie A, scoring 31 goals for Fiorentina, the highest scoring total in the league since 1959. He was trying to keep his incredible goal-scoring momentum against Ghana. A long ball was played into Italy's other starting striker, Alberto Gilardino, in the attacking third. Gilardino flicked the ball in the air to Toni, who headed the ball to himself around the defender, and blasted the ball at the goal. The shot was hit with such power that the goalie had no chance at stopping it, but fortunately for Ghana the ball smashed off the underside of the crossbar and stayed out of the net. Two inches lower and it would've been in for sure. Toni couldn't believe that his beautiful attempt was denied by the woodwork; the Ghanaians could breathe a sigh of relief.

The match approached halftime still scoreless. In the 40th minute, Italy had their tenth corner kick. The Italians had a series of corners to start the match, and the Ghanaian goalkeeper, Richard Kingston, looked a little shaky handling the swerving crosses. Lately he seemed to have gotten more comfortable, so Italy tried something different. Totti was set to take the corner kick, but instead of crossing it into the middle of the penalty area, he saw that his teammate Andrea Pirlo was open about 15 yards away. Totti played the ball on the ground to Pirlo who started to dribble towards the corner of the penalty area, about 25 yards away from the goal. There were still about 18 players in the penalty area that had been waiting for the cross. Pirlo could have tried to make a shorter cross to one of his teammates, but he must have been surprised by how much space he had and decided to try his luck at goal. The shot from Pirlo's right foot was perfect. Somehow the ball went untouched through a maze of players from both teams and right into the side netting. Italy went in front 1-0. The ball was within inches of three different players. If either of the defenders had deflected it, the shot would surely have missed. If Gilardino had grazed it with his head, he might have sent it wide. Unlike Toni's earlier attempt, Pirlo's shot was not even a fraction off target. Italy went into the locker room with the one-goal lead.

In the second half, trailing by a goal, Ghana was more aggressive. A powerful volley from Ghana's Michael Essien forced Italy's goalie Gigi Buffon into a great save. The shot was dipping towards the post when Buffon dove and used both his fists to punch it away. As Ghana continued to try and tie the game it opened up more opportunities for Italy to move forward. In the 67th minute, two midfielders moved into the attack for Italy as Daniele De Rossi slotted a perfect through ball to Simone Perrotta. Perrotta skipped around a sliding defender, teed up the ball and crushed a shot from close range, but the shot was too close to the goalie, and Kingston made a great reflex save.

Ghana continued to fight for the equalizer, but as they were forced to move players forward they may have overextended their own defense. For the second time in the match, Italy took advantage of what Ghana gave them. Pirlo played a long ball down the field for Vincenzo Iaquinta, who entered as a substitute in the second half. Pirlo's pass was not a great one, and it was easily intercepted by defender Samuel Kuffour, but Iaquinta was putting him under a lot of pressure. Kuffour decided to pass back to the keeper, but his pass was disastrous. He didn't pass it hard enough, and the charging Iaquinta quickly pounced onto the ball near the penalty area, dribbled around the stranded Kingston, and played the ball into the empty net. Italy went up 2-0 in the 83rd minute, ensuring the opening victory.

It's hard to tell if it was more from relief or excitement, but there was a huge celebration on the field after Iaquinta's goal. Players from the field and from the bench formed an enormous dog-pile on top of Iaquinta, who looked like he was nearly in tears before being engulfed by his teammates. The celebration was unusually grandiose for an early victory, but maybe the weeks of frustration and anxiety about all of the off-the-field issues leading up to the tournament were finally a thing of the past. After beating Ghana the players and coaches knew that it was possible for the team to focus on the matter at hand. The victory was worth much more than the three points in the standings.

After the first day of action in Group E, the Group of Death, Czech Republic was in first place with three points; Italy also had three points, but stood in second place because of goal differential. Ghana and U.S.A. each had zero points, with Team U.S.A. in last place since they lost by three goals. Everything can change in an instant in this tournament, and the Italians were by no means assured of moving on or avoiding Brazil, but for one night at least, Marcello Lippi and his players would sleep comfortably. The following morning it was back to work.

8

Italy 2–Ghana 0

When Iaquinta scored off the terrible and wonderful mistake from the Ghanaian defender, there was a raucous cheer that sprang forth from all of us watching the game. The loud yells from the adults were quickly followed by the scared screams of the three little ones. I was holding Lorenzo whose little face was contorted and turning red. I laughed because he was still cute, and also because Italy was going to win. Plus, he would be fine in a second. I looked back at the TV to see Iaquinta sliding on his back and his happy teammates piling on top of him. I thought, "That's probably just what Lorenzo needs!" I set him down on the floor facing the ceiling and lay down on top of him. He didn't seem to like that either. Well, now that we could watch the last few moments of the game without maximum concentration, I had to tend to my son.

There was one magical foolproof way to get these young cousins to cheer up. It seemed like no matter what the problem or crisis they were facing was, one song always lifted their spirits and sent them into an uncontrollable dance. It was very fitting that the song in question is a Neapolitan classic—Funiculì, Funiculà. The CD went on, the kids all started waving their arms around in delight, and their fears and confusion were gone as quickly as their ice cream for dessert. The babies were happy, and we all were happy; Italy won 2-0! It was peaceful on that Monday evening, but even though the sky was sunny, there were some dark clouds on the horizon: Italy against the United States.

In the days between the Ghana game and the U.S. game there were 12 other tournament games that were played. I watched all of them. During one broadcast (I forget the specific match), the two announcers started to comment on the teams that could potentially win the whole tournament. The announcer asked the analyst if Italy had a chance to become World Cup champions. His response was the following, "No, quite frankly." The announcer went on to say that Italy didn't have the quality of players that other teams did. He listed Argentina as his favorite to win it all. This expert's lifetime of acquiring soccer knowledge at the highest levels led him to believe that Team Italy could not win the World Cup. The term "expert" is used very liberally in the world of sports broadcasting.

I've already mentioned my rooting loyalties and my inner struggle with Ben Olsen, but as the buildup for the Italy–U.S.A. match mounted all week I realized that there was an American player even dearer to my heart than Olsen: Oguchi Onyewu. Oguchi was an up and coming American star. He was a central defender who left college early to earn a living playing soccer professionally in Europe. Germany 2006 was his first World Cup, and hopefully the first of several. Physically, Oguchi is an absolute specimen. If you ever see Greek sculptures of naked athletes you'll have some idea about Oguchi's physique. I'm sure that even the strongest-looking statue would ask for a robe if "Gooch" walked by with his shirt off. The physical presence of Oguchi was not the reason why I wanted him to succeed; it was because he was a longtime classmate, teammate, and childhood friend of my little brother Mikey.

Believe it or not I was at the first organized soccer game that Oguchi ever played in. The team was a collection of six-year olds. Oguchi was superior to all of the players on the field in terms of his speed and strength, but being a first grader he still needed a little work on his match awareness. Here's an example of what I mean. The purple team (that's Mikey and Oguchi's team) had a corner kick in the first half. The players all gathered in the penalty area. Pop (who was the coach) instructed Oguchi to go take the kick. Oguchi went over to the corner flag and looked back at the bench, seemingly needing more instruction. The assistant coach, John Dattoli, told him to kick it into the middle; simple but sound advice. Oguchi turned and blasted the ball towards the center circle, the middle of the field. There was a slight pause as the confused faces in the penalty area all turned and watched the ball roll far away from them towards midfield. Then they all collectively ran to chase the ball and the game continued.

Now, Oguchi had made it to the world's biggest stage. He had been a standout athlete all his life, separating himself from his remarkably athletic brothers and sisters. Pop had been his first coach, Pep had coached him later in elementary school when his CYO soccer team became the champion of the Mid-Atlantic region, and I had the good fortune of coaching him on Field Day when he was in eighth grade. We'd all known him since he was five, we'd all watched him grow up, and we were all very proud of everything he'd accomplished. It was hard to admit that now, in his biggest game ever, I wanted his team to lose. I think deep down I really wanted a tie.

At this point, I would like to mention one self-serving fact for my brother Mikey—on that CYO team that was the best on the East Coast, Mikey scored more goals than Oguchi.

With my tumultuous sea of emotions I don't know if I would have wanted to watch the match with my brothers, but fortunately I didn't have to decide for myself. On Saturday, June 17, it was match day two for Group E. Ghana played Czech Republic at 12 noon, followed by Italy vs. U.S.A. at 3 p.m. (all times Eastern). Also on that day, D.C. United was playing in New England at 6 p.m. The New England Revolution organization had made an excellent decision by opening the stadium doors hours earlier than normal to allow the fans to watch the U.S.A. game on the jumbo screen inside Gillette Stadium. It was a very cool idea and really the perfect way for the fans to watch the game. There I was, in my broadcast booth at Gillette Stadium, pulling for Italy but fully supporting Ben Olsen and Oguchi Onyewu. My paradox was complete and it seemed like a lose-lose situation.

9

Match Day 2—June 17
Italy vs. U.S.A.—Kaiserslautern

Things became very interesting on Saturday, June 17. The Group of Death lived up to its name. Ghana put forth an inspired effort in their second group match. They knew that another defeat would most likely send them out of the tournament, and they played like a team desperate for a victory. They began the game with a goal in the 2nd minute, played strong defense throughout, and had numerous chances in the second half before finally scoring the insurance goal for the 2-0 win. Both Italy and U.S.A. knew that the win for Ghana increased the stakes for their match. A win for Italy would put them with one foot in the next round; a win for U.S.A. would mean that all four teams in the Group of Death would be tied entering the final matches.

Team U.S.A. had suffered a disastrous defeat in their opening match, but after seeing the result from Ghana, they realized that three points for a win would be all the medicine they needed to get the loss to Czech Republic out of their system. The American coach, Bruce Arena, made some changes to his lineup to try and add more energy and firepower, two elements that were noticeably missing in their opener. For Marcello Lippi, there were also some adjustments, as players returned to full match fitness. Gianluca Zambrotta was in the starting lineup after missing the tournament opener. Zambrotta was an outside defender who was famous for excellent runs down the flanks.

He was an unusual defender who used great quickness moving into the attack, specifically with his slalom-type moves back and forth between opposing players. For Lippi he was a rare player who could help solidify a defense and add offense contemporaneously.

The match began with an aggressive start for the Americans. Team U.S.A. seized the initiative and had the Italians back on their heels at the outset. The Americans nearly took the lead in the 18th minute when a shot from Clint Dempsey zipped along the turf and went just inches wide of Buffon's far post. The Americans were desperate for the first goal, but instead it was the Italians who went in front. Italy had a free kick in the attacking third near the right sideline. Andrea Pirlo, the man of the match from Italy's opener, stepped up to take the kick. He curled a right-footed kick into the penalty area, and an unmarked Gilardino threw his body at the ball, connecting with a diving header that beat the U.S.A. goalie Kasey Keller and put Italy ahead 1-0 in the 22nd minute.

After the goal, Gilardino ran towards the end line, got down on one knee and began playing the air violin. It was unclear what the meaning was behind this gesture. Was it a tribute to a former music teacher? Was it to deride the Americans who had been complaining about poor officiating for the past four years? Was it to ensure himself a spot on highlight reels around the world? Whatever the reason, for Italian fans it was music to their ears.

The Americans were now in deep trouble. They'd conceded an early goal in their first match, and now they were behind once again. Fortunately for Team U.S.A., they managed to respond almost immediately. It was the most unfortunate of goals for Italy. U.S.A. earned a free kick near the corner flag. The American team captain, Claudio Reyna, sent a curling ball in towards the penalty area. A number of players went leaping for it, but it sailed over their heads. Italian defender Cristian Zaccardo was preparing to clear the ball away, but the players that had elevated for the ball created a diversion for him. Perhaps he lost sight of the ball for a split second, perhaps the flying bodies distracted him, but what happened next was disastrous. Zaccardo swung his left foot at the ball in an attempted clearance, but the ball glanced off the side of his foot and spun backwards towards his own goal. Buffon was positioned centrally and could do nothing but helplessly watch the ball roll across the goal line. The game was tied 1-1 on an *autogoal* from Zaccardo.

Suddenly there was hope for the Americans; for the first time in quite a while the U.S.A. had received a little bit of luck in the World Cup, and now Italy seemed to be somewhat shaken. Things went from bad to worse only moments later for Italy as midfielder Daniele De Rossi was given a red card for elbowing American forward Brian McBride in the face while going up for a header. De Rossi tried to convince the referee that it was accidental, but the television cameras caught the entire incident. The most memorable image of this match was McBride walking off the field with blood pouring down his face, and De Rossi was rightly sent off for the violent act. The foul was so egregious that it earned De Rossi a four-match suspension, meaning that his only chance to play again in the tournament would be if Italy made it to the final. Momentum was already in the corner of Team U.S.A., and now they had the advantage of playing 11 versus 10. There was over an hour left to play in the match, and Italy looked like a mere shadow of the team that was on the field against Ghana. Lippi needed to act to restore some order.

His act was a tactical one. He elected to use a substitution after only 35 minutes. Entering the match would be Gennaro Gattuso, a feisty defensive midfielder whose aggressive play is overshadowed only by his overall energy. Gattuso was sent in to replace Francesco Totti. Through the first half hour or so Totti had been nearly invisible. He wasn't totally invisible because everybody saw him receive a yellow card in the 5th minute. After that he had no impact. The substitution clearly indicated that Italy would be concentrating more on defending for the remainder of the match, a natural choice for Lippi since Italy was facing an uphill climb. It seemed like the immediate task for Italy was to make it into the locker room still tied at one.

About ten minutes after the sub, Italy nearly failed on that mission. American midfielder Pablo Mastroeni found some space near the top of the box and unleashed a vicious swerving shot that whistled just over the crossbar. It seemed as though Italy was living on borrowed time, but seconds before halftime, Mastroeni made another critical play. Andrea Pirlo was dribbling the ball near midfield, trying to move forward into the attack, but not doing so with any conviction. Mastroeni was in pursuit, and went sliding in with both feet, spikes up in the leg of Pirlo. Mastroeni missed the ball entirely, crunched into Pirlo, and was in big trouble with the referee. Mastroeni could have escaped with a yellow card, but the referee went straight for the red card. Some people believe the ref's decision was a make-up call to balance the sides once again, but the television replay showed the extent of the dangerous foul, and the referee's decision was not overly harsh. Momentum swung back to the Italians. At halftime the sides were even once again, in manpower and goals; Italy had 45 minutes to win this match and take control of Group E.

Two minutes into the second half Italy got another emotional boost. U.S.A. defender Eddie Pope was chasing Alberto Gilardino, who was dribbling towards the top of the box. Pope slid in from behind, missed the ball and brought down Gilardino. The referee reached into his pocket to give Pope a yellow card, but Pope had already received a yellow card in the first half. The second yellow sent the second American player for an early shower, and Italy would play nearly the entire second half ten players against nine.

Only five minutes after the second red card, the wheels nearly fell off for the Americans. Once again, Pirlo played a dangerous free kick into the penalty area. The ball was deflected and hit the crossbar. It was American defender Carlos Bocanegra who inadvertently sent the header towards his own goal. Italy nearly received an own goal after having already given up an own goal. In this match luck was with Bocanegra instead of Zaccardo.

The teams grew more and more tired as the game progressed. With fewer players on the field, there was more space, and consequently more running. Both coaches went to their benches to try and insert some fresh legs and fresh energy onto the field. The subs made immediate contributions. DaMarcus Beasley, perhaps the most gifted athlete on the American team, entered the game in the 62nd minute. Three minutes later, he accelerated into the penalty area and fired a low shot past Buffon and into the goal. The celebration had already begun for Team U.S.A., when they saw the assistant referee holding up his flag for offsides. Brian McBride was standing in front of Buffon in an offsides position, and even though Beasley's shot went straight into the goal without a deflection, the ruling was that McBride interfered with Buffon. The call was a frustrating one for the Americans but clearly the correct call, and the match remained tied.

For Italy, Alessandro Del Piero was the substitution that was the most likely to score the game winner. In the 73rd minute, Pirlo floated a beautiful pass into the path of Del Piero. The ball was just barely within the reach of Del Piero, who fully stretched out his left leg and managed to flick the ball towards the goal. The American goalie reacted very well and slapped the ball away. Six minutes later Del Piero tried his luck from long range. He managed to put a decent shot on target, but it ended up being a routine save for Keller. No game-winning goals for either side, and the match finished as a 1-1 draw.

Two down and one to go. The Group of Death was shaping up to be as difficult as anticipated. Group E was the only group in the tournament in which all four teams had the possibility to advance and all four of them could still be eliminated entering the final match day. After two matches, Italy sat in first place with four points from a win and a tie, Czech Republic and Ghana each had three points, and U.S.A. still had a fighting chance with their single point. The last day of play in Group E would be the day of reckoning for all four teams. In the Group of Death, the elimination round started early.

10

Italy 1–U.S.A. 1

There were two 1-1 ties that day, Italy–U.S.A. and D.C. United–New England. I was upset with both results, especially the Italy game. It's true that my original goal of both Italy and U.S.A. advancing from the Group of Death was more possible after their tie, but now Italy was more likely to be eliminated. During World Cup qualifying Italy had managed to secure their place in the final round well before the final match; there was no such luck this time. I'd have to sweat it out until the final whistle.

I don't really consider myself a sports fan. I like all sports, and I know a lot about many sports, but there are only two sports that affect my day-to-day existence: soccer and college basketball. Every March, NCAA basketball produces two of my favorite days of the year. They are the Thursday and Friday of the opening rounds of the NCAA Tournament. There are 16 games each day, and every one is significant. I love not having a day job so I can watch every moment. Match day three of the World Cup blows those days in March away. The groups are down to the final two matches, and the games within each group are played simultaneously. All the matches are broadcast live in the U.S., and one way that people monitor both games is to use the remote to switch back and forth between the games. Those people are FOOLS! There is only one way to watch the final matches of the group phase in the World Cup, the way I do it.

Meg and I own two TV's—one nice flat screen, and one smaller, older TV that normally is kept in our bedroom. Both TV's have their own cable box. For the four days of the World Cup when all the groups are decided, I take the TV from our bedroom (meaning that Meg can't fall asleep watching reruns of *Entourage*). The little TV—with cable box—moves down to the basement and is set up next to the big TV. I have a cable splitter which diverts the cable to the two screens so that they are both side by side with a cable hookup. Then, I put the game I am more interested in on the big TV with the second-rate game on the little TV. As soon as I turn on the TV's I quickly use the remote to change the channel of each TV to the channel showing the other game. That way all I have to do is hit the "LAST" button on the cable remote to instantly swap the two games. The little TV game goes to big TV, and vice-versa with the push of one button. The feature comes in very handy for goals, cards, key replays of the B-game, and also any time the A-game gets boring. One more "LAST" and the pictures are swapped back. It may sound a little extreme, but I promise if you do it next time you won't be able to go back to just one TV on those magical four days every four years.

In between the Italy–U.S.A. game and their final group match versus Czech Republic a large part of my family went to Germany for vacation. Pep, Kristen, Brigid, Alex, Nori, and Mikey were all in Germany to experience the World Cup in person. Even Gio was meeting up with them from Italy. They had tickets to some matches, but mostly they were going to be a part of the celebration and of course to "Make Friends" just as the tournament motto suggested. So, now that we could all cheer equally for Italy and U.S.A., half of my family had gone overseas. Johnny, who graduated from college a few weeks earlier, had recently started his new job, so he was not available to come to my house for the Italy–Czech game. It was a small gathering at my house, just Mom, Pop, Lorenzo and me. Normally Lorenzo and I would've gone to my parents' house, but since Pop thought I was crazy and refused to follow my advice about setting up the two TV's at his house, they drove the six minutes to my place. I don't remember him calling me crazy while he was watching the two matches simultaneously.

Everything was set, and the various possible outcomes really boiled down to two things. If Italy won and U.S.A. won, they would go through in first place and second place just as I had hoped. It wasn't quite that simple though because if Italy lost, then I would want U.S.A. to tie to ensure that Italy went through. The straightforward scenario got confusing very quickly. The one fact I was most concerned about was that if Italy won, they would go through in first place. To be honest, the U.S.A. victory would have been gravy. The games started just a few seconds apart; I don't think I need to tell you which game was on the big TV.

11

Match Day 3—June 22
Italy vs. Czech Republic—Hamburg

There were desperate teams throughout Group E on Thursday the 22nd. The two matches on the final day of group play were to be played simultaneously, so that no team could have the advantage of knowing ahead of time what result they needed. Italy knew that if they tied, they would advance to the second round, but if they tied and Ghana beat U.S.A., then Ghana would finish in first place in the group and Italy would face Brazil in their next game. From that point of view, you could expect Italy to go full throttle for the win, but if they overexerted themselves and lost to the Czech Republic, Italy could be eliminated from the tournament. It's the coach's job to make sure that the players are focused on the task at hand and not the myriad of different possibilities for advancement and elimination. For Lippi, the message to his team was loud and clear: three points today wins us the group.

Allegiances change very quickly in group play. Five days earlier, Italy and U.S.A. were entrenched in one of the fiercest battles of the entire tournament. Red cards, hard fouls, injuries, blood, cursing, and general ill will were all on display when those two teams went head-to-head. At the end of the match, neither team was pleased with the result, and both teams left the field with a palpable distaste for the other. Now, the players on Team U.S.A. were all Italy fans. U.S.A. was hoping with all their might that Italy would defeat the Czech

Republic, thus helping their own cause, while Italy was supporting a good effort from the Americans, since a tie between U.S.A. and Ghana meant that Italy only needed a tie to clinch first place in the group. Both games kicked off, and the ensuing two hours were as incident filled as any two-hour period in the lives of any player or coach from Group E.

In their previous match, Italy faced an American team that was very motivated after losing their last match. Now, in an even more important game, they would have to face another team fresh off an embarrassing defeat. Similar to the start of the U.S.A. game, Italy was put on the defensive immediately. There was a lot to motivate the Czech side on this day. The most obvious was that they were playing for their World Cup lives. The recent defeat also pushed them forward. It was clear that the Czechs were not intimidated by the Italians. Czech Republic was given an added boost as one of their best attacking players, Milan Baros, made his tournament debut. He was active from the first few minutes, and supported by the orchestration of Pavel Nedved, Czech Republic had dangerous scoring chances throughout the first quarter hour.

After 17 minutes, Italy suffered a key blow. One of their starting central defenders, Alessandro Nesta, who had played every minute of the first two games, was injured and forced to leave the game. Nesta had been a mainstay on the back line of the national team and is widely regarded as one of the best defenders in the world. For Nesta, the terrible luck of untimely injuries has been a theme throughout his career. In the 1998 World Cup he was injured in an opening round game and forced to sit out the remainder of the tournament. Such was to be his fate again eight years later. Entering in his place was the seldom-used Marco Materazzi. Materazzi is a very competent defender in his own right, but he has almost always been used as a backup to Nesta, earning the nickname "The Vice-Nesta." It seemed that under the current circumstances, Materazzi would have plenty of time to distinguish himself.

Twenty-two minutes into the Ghana match (remember, both games started at the same time) Ghana took the lead against U.S.A. The goal sent shockwaves through the group. If the results stayed the same (Ghana wins 1-0, Italy and Czech Republic tie 0-0), then Ghana would finish in first place and Italy would finish in second place. Even though the matches were being played in separate stadiums, news travels quickly, and the coaches are kept up-to-date. Four minutes after Ghana took the lead, another development in the group, from the Italy game. Italy scored to go in front 1-0. Francesco Totti sent a corner kick into the mixer where it was headed home by...Materazzi! Only eight minutes after coming in off the bench, Materazzi soared into the air, and snapped the ball down into the lower corner of the net for his first goal ever with the national team. It was a textbook finish. Group E had taken another dramatic turn; now if the scores stayed the same (Ghana wins 1-0, Italy wins 1-0) then Italy would go through first, and Ghana second.

Just before halftime there was a frenzy of significant activity from both games that changed the outlooks for all the teams several times. First, Team U.S.A. scored to tie that game at one. Clint Dempsey smashed a shot after a perfect pass from DaMarcus Beasley. The goal marked the first time all tournament that the Americans had actually scored a goal (their only other score was the own goal versus Italy). At that time, if the scores didn't change again (Ghana and U.S.A. tie 1-1, Italy wins 1-0) Italy would finish in first place and Ghana in second. Then, more news from the Italy match—Jan Polak committed a clumsy foul against Totti, earning his second yellow card. For the second straight match Italy would play with a man advantage. The Italy game went to halftime first, with the Italians still leading 1-0; then as the Ghana match entered stoppage time of the first half, Ghana was awarded a penalty. Ghana converted the kick and went into the locker room leading 2-1. With 45 minutes left, Italy was going through in first place and Ghana in second. There was exactly one half of a match left for U.S.A. and Czech Republic to change their fates.

The second halves both started without much incident. In the 60th minute Lippi brought in a substitute. Filippo Inzaghi made his debut in this World Cup. Inzaghi is a goal scorer, pure and simple. He has always had the uncanny, unteachable ability to put himself in the right place at the right time. In the 66th minute, America's Brian McBride sent a diving header off of the post. Team U.S.A. was running out of time, still needing two goals to advance to the next round. Italy continued to hold their one-goal lead, but a Czech goal would ensure that Ghana finished the group in first place. Italy still had a one-goal lead and a one-man advantage, making the job that much more difficult for the Czech Republic. The games were winding down. In the 87th minute came the knockout punch for Italy. A through ball from near midfield beat the Czech offsides trap and sent Inzaghi on a 50-yard breakaway. The only player on the attacking half besides Inzaghi was his teammate, another sub—Simone Barone. The two blue shirts raced towards the helpless keeper on a two-on-none break. Inzaghi dribbled all the way into the penalty area, and forced the goalie to commit. At this point, Inzaghi could have easily slid the ball to his teammate for a tap-in goal. But instead he did it all himself: dribbled around the 'keeper, played the ball into the net, collected his first World Cup goal ever, and sent Italy into the next round of the tournament as the winners of Group E. Should Inzaghi have passed to Barone? Probably. The goal would have been a much easier one for Barone, but "Super Pippo" gets paid to score goals, and since you never know if you'll get another chance to score in the World Cup, it's hard to blame him for being a little selfish.

In the other match, there was no dramatic finish; Ghana defeated U.S.A. 2-1 to wrap up second place in the group. U.S.A. and Czech Republic were both eliminated from the tournament, Ghana advanced in their first World Cup ever, and Italy finished in first place avoiding the round of 16 matchup with Brazil. Italy deserved a momentary respite to enjoy their early success and celebrate with their teammates and fans. The team could now enjoy the rest of the evening, knowing that they had accomplished their first goal. At this point they didn't know who their opponent would be, but it was better to not look ahead too soon. Nesta wouldn't be available and De Rossi continued to serve his long suspension for the red card against U.S.A. It was not the time to worry about the future; at this moment, confidence was higher than ever, and the frustrating tie against U.S.A. was water under the *Ponte Vecchio*. For Italian players and fans, the sky was as blue as the team jersey.

12

Italy 2–Czech Republic 0

Stage one: mission accomplished! I was happy for Pippo Inzaghi, who finally scored his first World Cup goal. When he decided not to pass to Barone I wasn't surprised, but I was appalled. Inzaghi scored, ran towards the corner flag, slid on both knees, and then fell face first on the ground. After that point I could finally breathe easy. I even changed the big TV to the U.S. game for the final few moments. I was so sad for Oguchi. The penalty that they called on him in some ways cost the U.S. the game and a place in the second round. I still believe that the referee made a mistake by giving the penalty, but I know that wouldn't make Gooch feel any better. Team U.S.A. went home as the last-place team in the Group of Death, but they were just a few critical plays away from going to the round of 16. Such is the peril of the World Cup.

I felt pretty bad for Alessandro Nesta too. It was unlikely that he would be able to play in the next game, and who knew how far Italy would go beyond that. Materazzi had filled in perfectly in the Czech game, but I didn't know how much longer he could keep it up.

After a three-hour lunch break, the afternoon session of games began and Italy would find out who their opponent would be: either Croatia or Australia. No matter which team progressed, there would be a lot of historic motivation for the Italian players—especially if they held grudges the way many Italians do. I've already expressed my anger and frustration about the 2002 World Cup, but I need to explain some specifics to understand the subtleties of the potential matchups in Italy's round of 16 match.

The referees were unusually bad during the 2002 World Cup. I have a number of key examples involving Team Italy, but I will begin with the most glaring error of the entire tournament, which happened in a game after Italy had been eliminated. I will begin with this mistake so that I come across as an open-minded observer instead of an Italy homer. The quarterfinal match between Korea and Spain went into golden goal overtime: sudden death. Late in the overtime, Spain was on the attack deep into the Korean end. A Spanish player dribbled all the way to the goal line and crossed the ball to a teammate near the far post who headed the ball in the goal. Spain was celebrating since they had just scored the goal to put them into the semifinal. There was one problem though: the linesman had his flag up, nullifying the goal. The assistant referee ruled that the ball had gone completely across the goal line before the player crossed it. Since the ball was already out, according to the linesman, the goal was disallowed and Korea was awarded a goal kick. Korea went on to win the match in a penalty shootout. The TV replays were perfectly clear—the ball was touching the line as the player crossed it, meaning that it was *NOT* out of bounds and the goal should have ended the match. The referees blew the call, destroyed the match, and sent Spain home as tragic underachievers once again.

Similar poor calls from the refs negatively affected Italy's 2002 tournament as well. In the group phase, Italy was paired with Croatia. On the second match day, Italy took the lead on Croatia before two goals from the Croatians three minutes apart had Italy in a desperate attempt to tie the match in the final seconds. On the last play of the match Marco Materazzi sent a long ball from near midfield high in the air towards the penalty box— it was soccer's form of a "Hail Mary" pass in football. The ball bounced in the crowded penalty area with nearly all the players battling to get to it. Amidst all of the pushing and tugging, the ball skipped past all the players and somehow wound up in the goal. It was a miraculous finish in which the Italians had managed an unthinkable tie. But the excitement was all for naught. The assistant referee had ruled that one of the Italian players had committed a foul, wiping away the goal. Inside the penalty area with nearly 20 players, 40 arms, and 40 legs all battling with one another, the linesman somehow saw an Italian being overly physical. Impossible. Italy lost the match and ended up finishing in second place instead of first.

Also in that match, Italy scored a goal which was called back for offsides. The replay showed that the officials had made a mistake in that decision as well. Finally, in the round of 16 game versus Korea, Italy had another goal taken away by an incorrect offsides call, and then another critical and horrible decision from the ref. In overtime, Italy was attacking into the heart of the Korea defense. A ball was played into the box to Francesco Totti, who was knocked over and fell to the turf. The referee immediately blew his whistle. Instead of awarding a penalty kick, the referee gave Totti a yellow card for diving. It was his second yellow card so he was ejected, and Italy allowed a golden goal while down a man to be eliminated from the tournament. Now, about that call on Totti. I don't know if it was a foul, but I know that it was *NOT* a dive. There was clearly contact from the defender, and even if it wasn't a foul, Totti was knocked over. I believe that the ref blew his whistle with the intention of giving Italy a penalty kick and changed his mind as he started to realize he might have made a mistake. At that point the ref had no option but to card Totti, and then he had to eject him. The referee, Byron Moreno of Ecuador, had a miserable performance, even worse than Italy's. Germany 2006 provided Italy with a chance to avenge the painful memories of the injustice of 2002.

If Italy was going to play Croatia, then they would have a chance to make up for that loss which cost them first place in the group four years earlier. If Italy was going to play Australia, then they would have a chance to make up for the Korea loss from four years earlier since the coach of Korea in 2002 was the coach of Australia in 2006. Basically, I watched the Croatia–Australia match hoping for a lot of red cards for both teams so that no matter who prevailed all of the most dangerous players would be suspended for the Italy game.

Australia only needed a tie to advance, and thanks to a late equalizer they managed to do it. There was also one red card to an Australian player; Brett Emerton received two yellows and was suspended for the Italy game. I felt confident against the Australians. I saw their qualifying playoff against Uruguay six months earlier, and I knew that they would certainly have the right attitude, but I liked Italy's chances, since we were stronger at every position on the field. When you get to the round of 16 all the teams are really talented, but relatively speaking I felt like Italy was in good shape; it was certainly a more favorable matchup than France–Spain or Portugal–Holland. There were no more easy games, but it was undeniably a good thing that we had avoided Brazil.

13

Round of 16—June 26
Italy vs. Australia—Kaiserslautern

Filippo Inzaghi's late goal versus the Czech Republic was the point at which even the most intense Italian fans could finally relax about winning Group E. Looking back, the second half of that game was pretty uneventful, as there were no real scares for the Italian team. For Italy's opponent in the round of 16 however, the second half in the Group F finale was the most important half in the soccer history of the two nations competing.

Brazil had taken a lead early in the second half against Japan and was on their way to wrapping up first place. At halftime of the other match being playing simultaneously, Australia and Croatia were tied at one. The winner of that match would advance to play Italy; if they tied, Australia would go through based on the tiebreakers. Australian coach Guus Hiddink had decided to start the backup goalkeeper Zeljko Kalac, even though he hadn't played yet in the tournament. In the 56th minute, Hiddink's decision looked like a catastrophic mistake. Croatian team captain Niko Kovac made a great run at the Australian defense, but his final shot was a weak one, moving slowly towards the Australian goalie. It's hard to explain what happened next. The ball went into the chest and arms of Kalac, and then somehow slipped or bounced over him and rolled meekly into the goal. It was the kind of unimaginable mistake that goalies rarely make. The shot had no business going in, as Kalac himself would admit, but on this occasion it did go in, and the Socceroos were down 2-1. Australia fought back, determined to not be eliminated from the tournament on their teammate's glaring error. Finally in the 79th minute, Australia's Harry Kewell scored to tie the match, sending Australia into the round of 16 for the first time in their nation's history and finalizing the date with Italy.

In 2002, Italy was eliminated from the World Cup by the co-host nation South Korea. The tragedy of the golden goal loss from four years earlier was still fresh on the minds of Italian fans. That defeat was considered by many to be one of the great upsets in World Cup history, and the mastermind who was the head coach of that Korean team was none other than the current coach of Australia, Guus Hiddink. Hiddink was looking to repeat his upset from 2002 and eliminate Italy in the round of 16 for the second straight World Cup. To do so, Hiddink would have to make sure the team was at full strength; naturally he re-inserted goalkeeper Mark Schwarzer into the starting lineup.

Italy began the match on the attack. Coach Lippi had decided that the creative midfielder Francesco Totti needed a little bit of a rest and started Alessandro Del Piero in his place. Less than three minutes into the match, Del Piero made his presence felt. He used a series of good skills near the corner flag and sent a dangerous cross into the penalty area. Luca Toni elevated well and sent a header inches wide of the post. About fifteen minutes later, Toni was involved once again, this time a long ball from near midfield was sent high into the box for him. Two defenders moved towards Toni, but this time instead of shooting, he headed back across the box to his open teammate Alberto Gilardino. The ball bounced on the ground in front of Gilardino, and he had to wait a moment to take his shot. When he did shoot it, the shot was right at Schwarzer, who easily tipped it over the crossbar.

Two minutes later, Toni had another excellent chance to put Italy in front. Andrea Pirlo sent a long ball into the box for Toni, this time with only one defender near him. Toni controlled the ball, shielded the defender, turned towards the goal from close range and sent a low shot to the goal. The entire maneuver happened in the blink of an eye. Schwarzer anticipated that Toni's shot would go to the far post and was already leaning that way as Toni struck the ball. Toni was actually aiming for the near post, and the Australian 'keeper had already committed to going the opposite way. Even though his momentum was going away from the ball, Schwarzer stuck his left leg out behind him and managed to deflect the shot away. It was an incredible save.

In the 30th minute, Australia had a free kick at the top of the attacking third. The ball was played into the penalty area and deflected high into the air by the Italian defense. The ball was dangerously coming back down in the box with a group of players all battling for it. The ball caromed and was then rolling slowly across the box. The first player to react to it was Australia's Scott Chipperfield. From close range he blasted a low shot towards Buffon, who made a fantastic save and quickly pounced on the short rebound. Thanks to the excellent work of both goalies, the game entered halftime zero-zero.

Early in the second half, Australia was surging forward as Marco Bresciano tried to slip through the back line of the Italian defense. As he approached the penalty area, Marco Materazzi went sliding in to try and tackle the ball. Materazzi missed the ball, Bresciano went tumbling over Materazzi's legs, and the referee rightly called a foul on the Italian. The Spanish referee Luis Medina Cantalejo reached into his pocket and pulled out a card—a red card. Materazzi couldn't believe it. Realizing there was no point in arguing his helpless case he waved his arm dismissively at the ref and slowly made his way to the locker room.

Once again, Lippi's hand was forced. Andrea Barzagli, the third-string central defender who hadn't played in the entire tournament, was quickly summoned off the bench to compensate for the loss of Materazzi (the original starter, Nesta, was still out with injury). The 25-

year-old defender from Palermo was sent into the game to replace Luca Toni. Toni, who was the most dangerous player on the field in the first half, never had a chance to get going in the second half. Italy was now playing down a man, without their best attacking player, and with an inexperienced central defender making his World Cup debut. Fortunately, the Italians still had Cannavaro and Buffon.

Australia took advantage of the extra player and began to control the possession. Only eight minutes after the red card, the Socceroos strung together a series of good passes, culminating in a clear shot on goal for Chipperfield. He blasted a shot from about ten yards, but as always Buffon was positioned perfectly and punched the attempt away. Australia continued to knock on the door for most of the second half, but the organized Italian defense kept the match scoreless.

In the 75th minute Lippi used his final substitution, bringing in Francesco Totti to replace Del Piero. Ideally, Totti was supposed to provide a spark, and possibly connect with the first substitute Iaquinta to try and steal a late goal. It would be a very difficult task with only ten men. As the match entered the final 15 minutes, Australia was certainly the team more likely to score. Besides the circumstances of the current game, they had a very good recent history of late match heroics: they qualified for the World Cup by winning a penalty shootout, they scored three goals in the final eight minutes of their World Cup opener versus Japan, and they scored in the 79th minute against Croatia to advance to this stage. The chances kept coming for Australia, but they couldn't manage to break down the Italian defense, which apparently was slightly stronger than Japan's. Into stoppage time, the game was still without a goal. The Italian defenders seemed ready to make sure the match would get to extra time, but then one Italian defender made sure it didn't.

Fabio Grosso was a rather unknown player for Team Italy. He didn't play for one of Serie A's top clubs like Juventus, AC Milan, Inter, or Roma; he played for Palermo. He wasn't as famous as Fabio Cannavaro or Alessandro Nesta, he wasn't as creative as Gianluca

Zambrotta, but he made the most critical play of Italy's World Cup run to date. In the third minute of stoppage time, with both teams exhausted from the heat and the 90 minutes of competition, the match was moments from overtime.

In the final seconds, Totti had the ball in the center circle. He slowly moved back and forth looking for a passing lane, but all of the Australians were perfectly spread out across the field denying any angles. The Australians didn't move toward Totti to try and get the ball; they just all moved side to side as Totti did to make sure the final whistle blew and the teams could regroup. It was comical how much the scene resembled a foosball table. At last, partly from desperation and partly from optimism, Totti sent a long ball high in the air down the left sideline.

Grosso and the Australian Marco Bresciano were both waiting for the ball to come down. Grosso made a subtle play to win the ball. He faked as though he would take the ball centrally, but then let the ball bounce and moved with it down the sideline. The move was effective, as he had managed to control the ball while advancing towards the attacking third; Bresciano was still right alongside. The two moved towards the corner flag when Grosso quickly cut inside the defender and angled his way to the penalty area. As Grosso went past Bresciano, their legs got tangled up and Bresciano lost his balance and fell down. Now Grosso was inside the penalty area, wide open from a sharp angle. Grosso had some teammates in the box and was considering centering the ball. The closest defender for Australia was Lucas Neill, who went sliding at Grosso to try to block an attempted cross, but instead of passing, Grosso cut the ball back and collided with the body of the sliding defender, tumbling on top of him to the turf. As the two players lay entangled on the ground, the world stopped. The 92,000 eyes of the spectators in the stadium saw what had happened; they saw the great run from Grosso, they saw the risky slide tackle from Neill, they saw Grosso fall to the ground in the penalty area, and at that point everything froze. Finally, the universe resumed with the whistle of the referee, who was holding out his arm and pointing at the penalty spot.

The magnificent run from Fabio Grosso had set up a scenario that seemed impossible just eight seconds earlier: Italy had a chance to win the match in the final seconds from the penalty spot. Francesco Totti stepped up to the ball with a chance to put Italy into the quarterfinals. Schwarzer waited on his goal line, trying to calm his nerves and make the greatest play in Australian soccer history. The referee blew the whistle. Totti approached the ball. He struck it with his right foot. The ball moved towards the goalie's right. Schwarzer dove to his right. The ball whizzed past the outstretched fingers of the goalie and into the back of the net. Italy took the lead 1-0.

Totti immediately started sucking his thumb and smiling, sending a coded message of "*Ti voglio bene*" back to his young child at home. As Totti ran in celebration towards the corner of the stadium, the first player there to leap into his arms was the player he replaced in the lineup back in the 75th minute, Alex Del Piero. The image of the two players who compete for the same starting position in a euphoric embrace was an image of the purity of the game. There were no egos or personal agendas on display, just two players on the same team, elated to be moving on to the next round of the world's most important tournament. In many ways the vision of Totti and Del Piero represented this Italian team as a whole—every individual working together for the sake of the group, and thrilled with the success of the group.

The goal from Totti was scored so late in the match that the Australians didn't even have the opportunity to kick off. It's very unusual for a soccer match to end without the other team at least having a desperation attempt to score in the dying seconds, but that was the case on this occasion. Italy's goal celebration took them directly into the locker room, where they met up with a much-relieved Materazzi.

Italy had made it through to the quarterfinals in one of the most fantastic finishes of the nation's storied history. The dramatic final seconds against Australia conjured images of the 1994 World Cup, when an Italian team also playing with ten men in the round of 16 managed to score a game-tying goal in the final seconds, and then went on to win in overtime. On that day it was Roberto Baggio whose two goals against Nigeria re-affirmed his world superstar status. As for Fabio Grosso, he had quite a way to go before being compared to Baggio, one of the greatest players in Italian soccer history, but for the moment he was enjoying his time in the sun.

Back home in Italy the Vespas were already zipping around the piazzas from the Veneto to the Basilicata. The Italian people who live and die with *Gli Azzurri* knew the importance of the match. These knowledgeable fans understood the difficulty of playing for so long with only ten men. They knew how unlikely it is to score a goal when the opposition has an extra player. They also knew, perhaps most importantly, that their opponent in the quarterfinals would be a relatively easy one, either Ukraine or Switzerland. About four hours into the celebrations going on throughout Italy, the other round of 16 match ended. After 120 minutes of scoreless play, Ukraine defeated Switzerland in a penalty shootout. Switzerland missed all of their attempts in the shootout, failing to kick the ball into the goal at any point during the two-and-a-half-hour-long display of attacking futility. The quarterfinal was set: Italy vs. Ukraine.

14

Italy 1–Australia 0

Lorenzo and I went to Pop's house to watch the Italy–Australia game. Those other people were still all in Germany, and Mom was too nervous to watch once Materazzi was sent off. I remember being very frustrated and nervous in the final seconds of that match, and when Grosso made the critical play I remember seeing the referee give an overly dramatic point to the penalty spot and I remember both Pop and myself screaming in unison. It was a win that provided an excellent adrenaline rush. Italy had snatched a victory from the jaws of overtime, and in my experience, draining, dramatic victories like that one can really propel teams forward.

I'm always amazed at how everything in a person's life can change in a mere instant. At the start of the Australia game Italy was flying. Luca Toni was a total menace, and it was just a matter of time before he scored. Then the red card to Materazzi and the Australians were sure to go in front. Finally the incredible play by Grosso and millions of Australians were totally crushed. It's unbelievable.

While we were still celebrating, the phone rang; Nori was calling long-distance from Kaiserslautern. She and Gio had managed to get tickets to the game and were just making their way out of the stadium. It was very loud in the background and she was saying how awesome it was. I thought it was awesome watching from across the world; I can't imagine what it would've been like to be there in person. She said that there were so many Australian fans, and they were all so quiet after the goal. Then she added, "Ha, ha!" Nori has always been very sympathetic.

A little while after we hung up with Nori, I decided to call Johnny. He had just started working about a week earlier at his new job. He had the ability at work to check the score online, but I wanted to make sure he got the whole story. As it turned out, Johnny actually was able to watch most of the second half on his lunch hour. He was out with a few of his new coworkers and his boss. The other men got up to leave the restaurant just as Italy was awarded the penalty kick. Johnny looked around wondering if he should tell them to wait until after the kick, or if he should just do what they did. Johnny managed to delay a little bit behind them, saw Totti make the kick, and then still made it to the car in time to ride back to the office. I'm not sure exactly why the rest of Johnny's coworkers didn't wait the extra 90 seconds or so, but it all worked out okay and Johnny didn't offend the boss.

A few hours after the Italy game, the match was played to determine Italy's opponent. The reward for Italy's hard-fought victory was a free pass to the semifinals. Italy would either play Switzerland or Ukraine, and neither one stood a chance against Italy. As it turned out, the Switzerland–Ukraine game ended up being the exact game that people who don't like soccer point to when saying that soccer is dull. Ukraine won in a penalty shootout and earned the right to lose to Italy in the quarterfinals. I had never been more confident about an Italian World Cup elimination match, and that includes watching reruns of classic matches when I already knew the outcome.

That was a busy week for me. The Italy game was on Monday. On Tuesday I had a busy day of watching two more World Cup round of 16 matches (Brazil beat Ghana and France beat Spain). On Wednesday morning I flew to Kansas City to broadcast a D.C. United game. On Thursday my people came home from Germany. On Friday was the Italy vs. Ukraine match. Let's go back to Wednesday and go into more detail.

In Kansas City, Missouri, D.C. United defeated the Kansas City Wizards 3-2. At the team hotel after the match I was speaking with two D.C. United players, Facundo Erpen and Christian Gomez, both of whom are Argentinean. The winner of the Italy–Ukraine game would face the winner of the Germany–Argentina game in the semifinals. I asked them (in Spanish) if they thought the foul on Grosso should have been a penalty kick. They both said that it was definitely *NOT* a penalty and the Italians were lucky. Slightly changing the subject I asked if we could still be friends even if Italy played Argentina in the semifinal. They responded that Argentina would have a really tough game against Germany, but of course they could be friends with me; since Argentina would beat Italy for sure, it was more a matter of if I could still be friends with them. They were both friendly, but a little too smug for me, especially Facundo. I asked if Germany beat Argentina, could Italy beat Germany. Facundo pretended to think about it briefly and then said, "Italia…no."

Then they started to talk about how they were against the Italians because of the way the Argentina national team was treated during the 1990 World Cup held in Italy. Argentina had advanced to the final match by beating Italy in a penalty shootout in the semifinals. Their opponent was Germany. During the pre-game ceremony, almost the entire stadium in Rome was booing and whistling throughout the playing of the Argentina national anthem. Some accounts say that the rude behavior was led by an incredibly large contingent of German fans who had crossed the border into Italy to attend the game, but Christian and Facundo (and probably many other Argentineans) held the Italians responsible. I didn't remember the incident during the national anthem, but since our conversation I have seen highlights of it, and it is strange to see how the players on the field looked sad and offended at the distasteful reaction from the crowd. I don't blame the Argentineans for being bitter.

After that we talked a little more about the World Cup, and World Cups past. The more we talked the more I realized that they were crazy fans just like me. Christian and Facundo were good players, but compared to the best players in Argentina, they were just as likely as I was to make a World Cup roster. Here were these professional soccer players that turned into little kids when talking about their favorite players and their favorite team. At that point I thought it would be better for everybody if Italy didn't play Argentina in the semifinals—so that the three of us wouldn't harbor any bad feelings towards the other. There was another reason why I didn't want Argentina to play Italy—Argentina was probably the most talented team in the tournament!

I returned to BWI Airport Thursday morning and later that afternoon my family who had been vacationing in Germany arrived at Dulles Airport. We all had a nice dinner together while they told us a lot of great stories about their trip. On the day of the Italy–Australia match, everyone who didn't go to the game was hanging out in a Fan Fest area ready to watch the match on an enormous TV screen. The twins were wearing replica Italy uniforms, jerseys, and shorts (they would've worn the socks too but those were sized to fit eight-year-olds). An Italian photojournalists took some pictures of them and used them on the website of one of the famous Italian sports newspapers. Brigid and Alex were both celebrities at 17 months old. They had come back bearing gifts as well. For Lorenzo they brought a small soccer ball. On each of the 32 panels of the ball there was painted the flag of one of the 32 World Cup nations in the tournament along with the country's name in German. Nori brought me a souvenir from the Australia game. It was a T-shirt with the Italian flag and the Australian flag along with the date of the game and the name of the venue. It was a great shirt, but I didn't want to wear it yet. If Italy went out of the tournament then I could wear the shirt and look back with happiness on that game. But as long as Italy was still in the tournament I didn't want the Australia match to be the high point. I kept the shirt in my closet, hoping that I wouldn't want to wear it for three more games.

My family had to shake off any jet lag pretty quickly, because the day after they arrived back in the U.S. was Italy's next match. For this match we had two extra people in our already crowded family room, a pair of teenage sisters from Italy named Anna and Laura. They were cousins of ours who were spending a month in the United States studying English and living with my parents.

As I mentioned in an earlier chapter, my father was born in Italy. Specifically he was born in Naples. My grandfather left many family members behind, including some siblings, when he departed for the United States. Pop still had first cousins living in Italy. Through a number of amazing benefits from Pop's job, we were all able to travel to Italy many times in our youth absolutely free of charge. Yes, all of the travel for Mom and Pop and all of their kids was totally paid for by my father's employer, the International Monetary Fund. We went to Italy about every three years from the time Pep was born until we each in turn celebrated our 23rd birthdays. Once you turned 23, the free transportation turned back into a pumpkin.

Thanks to these trips, we all became unusually close to the relatives we have near Naples. The small town outside of Naples is called Castellamare di Stabia, located right on the Bay of Naples. The town itself is as pretty as its name. In this town there is a very close-knit family whose grandmother was the sister of my grandfather. The close-knit family I mentioned consists of three sisters and three brothers. My brothers and sister have always had a very special bond with these cousins. We only saw them every three years during our summer vacations, but it seemed like every time we returned there, it was like we had never left. These wonderful people had a way about them that put you immediately at ease, and we all consider ourselves very lucky to have been so fully included into their loving family. Their family is almost as crazy about soccer as ours is.

In 1994 we were all in Italy during the World Cup. It's a little ironic that in the year when the World Cup was actually taking place in Washington, D.C., we were watching most of the matches in Italy with these cousins. During the 1994 World Cup Italy marched all the way to the finals. In their round of 16 match they needed a last-second goal to force overtime. We were watching that game in Italy. When Italy managed to somehow escape with that victory, the town went totally haywire. Every Vespa in the town was zipping around the piazza, Italian flags waved everywhere, and people were screaming and blasting horns from the windows of their homes. I had never seen anything like it. It reminded me of old news reels I had seen when World War II ended. Words can never do justice to the experience of witnessing the scene that night. I was honored to be a part of it, and it was another way in which the special bond between our family and theirs grew stronger. Anna and Laura are the great-granddaughters of my grandfather's sister. Italy had never lost a World Cup match when I was on Italian soil, and I thought that the same good luck might exist since these girls were here with us. We wouldn't need luck against Ukraine though.

15

Quarterfinals—June 30
Italy vs. Ukraine—Hamburg

Just when it seemed like things might finally be going Italy's way, there was another grave distraction from home. The investigation of the corruption in Serie A continued to intensify. Juventus remained at the center of the accusations. Five players on the national team played for Juve during the past season: Gianluigi Buffon, Mauro Camoranesi, Fabio Cannavaro, Alessandro Del Piero, and Gianluca Zambrotta.

A former player for Juventus and the Italian national team, Gianluca Pessotto, who had just been moved into the front office of Juventus, was found on the ground outside the team headquarters building, critically injured after falling from the fourth floor. Some of the national team players left Germany to return home and visit him in the hospital. It was unclear whether the fall was a suicide attempt or not, but Pessotto was found with a rosary clutched in his hands. The pressure and intensity of the investigation was mounting, but the Italian players needed to find a way to regain focus on their quarterfinal opponent.

Ukraine's arrival in the quarterfinals was totally unexpected after their first match of the tournament when they lost to Spain 4-0. The good news for the Ukrainians was that Spain was by far the most difficult team in the group. Ukraine avenged their opening defeat with a 4-0 victory over Saudi Arabia and finished group play with a 1-0 victory over Tunisia on a questionable penalty kick earned and converted by Ukraine's most dangerous attacking player, Andriy Shevchenko. The Ukrainians played one of the most boring matches of the entire tournament in their round of 16 match versus Switzerland, but it was a joyous occasion in the end as the PK shootout sent the Eastern European nation into the quarterfinals in their first World Cup ever. They would need to put together a better performance to beat Italy.

Totti was back in the starting lineup, now playing as a retracted striker, meaning that he was playing behind the only true striker on the field for Italy, Luca Toni. For the second match in a row, Italy started the game surging into the attack. There were near misses for Italy in the opening moments of the Australia match, but on this day their first clear chance did not miss.

Gianluca Zambrotta had the ball at the midfield line near the right sideline. He passed a ball forward on the ground to Totti and started to surge forward for the return pass. As the pass rolled to Totti, the Ukrainian defender was right up against him. Totti didn't have time to collect the ball and make a pass, so he quickly used his heel to one-touch the ball back to the streaking Zambrotta. The pass surprised the Ukrainians, and was perfectly in stride for Zambrotta, who quickly took two more dribbles, rapidly approaching the penalty area. Usually when he gets towards the penalty area he looks to pass to one of his teammates. This time however, he went for glory himself. He struck the ball with his left foot and sent a low shot towards the corner of the goal which glanced off the fingers of the Ukrainian 'keeper and gave Italy the lead 1-0. The sixth-minute goal was the fastest of the tournament for the Italians, and Zambrotta, who works so tirelessly and does so many of the little things for Italy, was rewarded with only his second goal ever for the national team. He couldn't hide his excitement, leaping high into the air with an energetic fist pump and a big smile on his face. Zambrotta didn't know it at the time, but he was on his way to his greatest game ever with the national team. The fast start was important for Italy, but it didn't result in an easy match. There weren't many good chances for either team through the rest of the first half, and it looked as though the Ukrainians were content to have reached this stage of their first World Cup.

To start the second half, Ukraine was the aggressor. Whatever transpired in the locker room at the intermission gave a shot in the arm to the Ukrainians, who for the first time in the match seemed poised to tie the score. Five minutes into the second half Ukraine managed their first real threat. With many players moving forward, Anatoliy Tymoschuk sent a dangerous cross from the right sideline in towards the far post. The cross swerved away from Buffon and found Andriy Gusin, who snapped a header towards the ground at the post. Buffon reacted very well to make the save, but in doing so he collided head first into the goal post. Buffon was grimacing and clearly shaken up from the knock to his head, but having come this far in the tournament he wasn't about to be taken out of the match.

Eight minutes later, the Ukrainians were within inches of scoring. Oleg Gusev managed to break through the last line of defense and found himself one-on-one with Buffon from only a few yards away, but at a very wide angle. Gusev tried to blast the shot past Buffon, who made another critical save, blocking the shot with his fists, and sending the rebound out into the box. Many Italian defenders, including Zambrotta and Cannavaro, were racing to the goal to try and get back into position. The rebound from Buffon deflected off his teammate Cannavaro and fell to Maksym Kalinichenko, who blasted a shot towards the goal. Buffon was still out of position from his initial save and was scrambling to make his second save in a row. It would have been interesting to see if Buffon, who had played flawlessly all tournament, would have been able to save the rebound attempt from Kalinichenko. Fortunately for the Italians, he didn't have to.

For generations, the Italians have been perfecting the art of defense. For most people, this style of play is not very entertaining and somewhat boring, but in critical situations during matches, there is no way to overestimate the value of the art of defending. Just as the Brazilians and the Dutch show such creative instincts on the ball with individual skills and moves, the Italians understand innately the angles and positioning to defend impeccably. These instincts kicked in during this frantic flurry for the Ukrainians.

Gusev had the best chance to score for Ukraine; he was momentarily open in the penalty area, which is all that an attacking player can hope for versus Italy. Once Buffon made that initial save, there were six Italian defenders who had recovered to help sort out the situation. Cannavaro, Camoranesi, Barzagli (who started in place of the suspended Materazzi), Grosso, Pirlo, and Zambrotta were all clogging up the six-yard box. Kalinichenko had to rush his shot due to the pressure from Cannavaro and Pirlo, and even though he did well to keep the shot on target, there was another defender waiting in perfect position to block the shot on the goal line, just in case Buffon didn't make it over in time. Gianluca Zambrotta made his second critical play of the match, as he lowered his body to block the ball away. He did so with his arms at his sides, avoiding any chance for a handball and a penalty kick. The Italian defense had refused to break down, and the emotional lift from the superb team defensive effort was rewarded by the attacking players just seconds later.

The Italians nearly lost their slim one-goal lead and decided it was time to double it. Italy had a corner kick, and Francesco Totti played it short to a teammate, quickly receiving the return pass. Then from near the left corner flag, Totti sent a curving cross into the penalty box, where Luca Toni headed the ball into the goal for the 2-0 lead. It was the first goal of the tournament for Luca Toni, and the combination of Totti and Toni had given their flawless defenders more breathing room than they needed. Toni had a huge smile on his face as he celebrated his goal with his usual gesture of cupping his right hand near his ear to let the fans know that he wanted to hear them even louder. This goal was Italy's eighth of the tournament, and incredibly it was scored by the eighth different player. Once again, the importance of the team was highlighted, with so many essential contributions coming from so many different players. The attack was powerful and had so many different options, the defense was solid no matter which players comprised the back line, and the goalkeeping was magnificent. There was no way that Italy would lose the two-goal lead. In the 59th minute, Italy was through to the semifinals.

Ukraine continued to cling to a sliver of hope. Three minutes after falling behind 2-0 they had another good scoring opportunity. Again it was a Gusin header that was fractionally off the mark; he managed to beat Buffon for once, but the ball clanged off the crossbar. That was the final opportunity for Ukraine. In the 68th minute, Marcello Lippi made a double substitution, inserting the seldom-used Simone Barone as well as Massimo Oddo, who had yet to play in this World Cup. When Oddo entered the match, it meant that every player on Lippi's roster (with the exception of the two backup goalkeepers) had played in at least one match. The use of the entire field roster may seem like a trivial note, but it shows the respect that Lippi had for all of his players, even the 23rd man on the roster. Lippi's use of Oddo was a clear example of the togetherness of this team and the emphasis placed on the value of each individual within the context of the team. Later in the match Cristian Zaccardo came off the bench as the final substitute, making his first appearance since the game against Team U.S.A. Electing to give Zaccardo another chance on the field so that his final World Cup match wouldn't be one in which he scored an own goal was yet another display of unity and respect from Lippi.

In the 69th minute, Italy brought down the curtain on Ukraine. Gianluca Zambrotta capped off his majestic game with another run at the defense. The ball was played into Zambrotta near the intersection of the goal line and the edge of the penalty area. Zambrotta quickly cut the ball back centrally and split two defenders. Then, as he approached the goal area he attracted two other players and the goalie, at which point he slid a perfect pass to the center of the goal where Luca Toni was eagerly waiting to collect his second goal of the match and establish the final score line as 3-0. Toni celebrated for the second time encouraging the noise from the crowd, and back home in Italy thousands of fans poured into the streets trying to make sure that he could hear their screams of joy all the way in Germany.

Thanks to his usual intensity and menacing ways in the midfield, Gennaro Gattuso, the fire bolt, sparkplug, bundle of aggression and energy, was named the man of the match. Gattuso was the man of the match, but Zambrotta was the hero of the match. He scored his first World Cup goal, which held up as the game winner, he cleared a shot off of his own goal line when the match was still in the balance, and he set up the final goal which sent Italy emphatically into the semifinals. There was only one bit of unfinished business for Zambrotta. After the final whistle blew and the Italian team was celebrating on the field, Zambrotta and Cannavaro had a heartfelt message to display to the world. They were walking on the field holding an Italian flag between them. Written in big blue letters across the flag was the message *"Pessottino Siamo con te"* – *To our Buddy Pessotto, We're all with you.* In the most exhilarating moment of their professional careers, the members of this unified team still had the presence of mind to send their well wishes to their former teammate Gianluca Pessotto, recovering in a hospital back in Italy.

The obvious expressions of humility continued for the Italian team. No one player was more important than any other. The joy and enthusiasm that was shared within this group were among the most important reasons for the success of this team. There were many obstacles that the squad encountered: injuries to key players, suspensions at inopportune times, the impending findings of the corruption investigations, and the near death of a close friend. But in spite of all the adversity, the team grew stronger, more unified, and more confident. *Gli Azzurri* had steamrolled their way into the World Cup semifinals, a place they hadn't been since the Baggio-led team of 1994. Italy was only one match away from their sixth appearance in the World Cup final, but the team that stood in their way would bring much more of a challenge than Ukraine. Italy vs. Ukraine was a standard 11-on-11 matchup; in the semifinal, Italy would be playing against 65,000 opponents.

16

Italy 3–Ukraine 0

Anytime a team is trying to win a tournament, the fans look to previous tournaments for guidance; it's only natural. Italy last won the World Cup in 1982, so for Italians, any similarities between this team and the team from 1982 would give confidence and hope to current fans. In 1982, Paolo Rossi was the goal-scoring hero for the Italians. He started the tournament scoring zero goals in his first four matches and then erupted for three goals in the quarterfinal, two more in the semifinal, and one in the final. Luca Toni entered the 2006 World Cup as Italy's most dangerous scoring threat, but after his first four matches, he had scored zero goals. When Toni scored the final goal against Ukraine, his second of the match, the Italian announcer started repeatedly yelling, "Luca Toni, just like Paolo Rossi!" The similarities were clear, and if Toni could add a hat trick down the line you could bet that Italy would repeat the feat of 24 years earlier. First and foremost I wanted that to happen, but since it wasn't very likely, I was just a little disappointed that he had scored twice.

Up until the third goal versus Ukraine, Italy had scored eight goals. Eight different players had scored the goals. Before the quarterfinal Pep and I were talking, and I told him, "I hope Italy wins the World Cup with no player scoring more than one goal." We briefly went over the possibilities looking at the roster. Prior to the start of the Ukraine game, Italy had scored six goals, and the six goal scorers were Pirlo, Iaquinta, Gilardino, Materazzi, Inzaghi, and Totti. Clearly Luca Toni would eventually score, and so would Del Piero. We could maybe get one goal from Perrotta or Camoranesi since they play so much, and then the fitting game-winning goal in the final could come from the team captain, Cannavaro. It was just as likely as Italy winning the World Cup. When Zambrotta scored to make it 1-0, I yelled to Pep, "He's not even on our list!"

As the match ended, Funiculì, Funiculà burst forth from the CD player. Anna and Laura joined in and were amazed at how cute and coordinated the three babies were. For this match Mom had taught Lorenzo a new trick. Now that Italy was officially in the semifinals it was time for everybody to be at their best.

Lorenzo had gotten into the habit of waving his finger like a conductor when music was played; whether it was Brahms' lullaby or Ricky Martin. Mom had tried to explain to Lorenzo about the games and about cheering for Italy; I think Lorenzo was learning to clap too. Mom taught Lorenzo to wave his finger when she cheered for Italy. Mom would say, "I-TAL-IA, I-TAL-IA" and Lorenzo would start to wave his finger like when fans yell, "We're Number One! We're Number One!" It was very cute, and it was a nice wrinkle to the already joyous celebration.

Now there was only one team standing in the way from Italy getting to the World Cup championship match—Germany. I remember many years ago talking with my cousin Nicola; he is Anna and Laura's uncle. We were talking about the World Cup and he started talking about how Italy always beats Germany. He seemed to love talking about it and was almost giddy throughout the conversation. I think that he might've been a little smug, like my Argentinean friends Facundo and Christian were when they talked about Argentina. Historically, Nicola was perfectly right. Germany had never beaten Italy in the World Cup, but I didn't think that the Germans would just forfeit the game since history was against them. I was sort of hoping they would.

Throughout the tournament my family had been spread out in different parts of the world. Because of jobs, vacations, and school we hadn't watched a full match all together the entire tournament. The trend would continue in the semifinal. I couldn't watch the game with everybody else since D.C. United had a road game the day of the semifinal. Well, if everything went according to plan I would have one last chance to watch one last Italy game with everybody. That was a big if.

17

Semifinals—July 4
Italy vs. Germany—Dortmund

Italy's quarterfinal victory was the most comfortable margin of victory of the four teams that advanced into the semifinals. Italy's potential opponents were Argentina and Germany, and those two nations played a fascinating match. There was a storied history between the two nations. They had met in consecutive World Cup final matches in 1986 and 1990, with each side taking the crown once. In the 2006 edition of the storied matchup, Argentina scored the game's first goal early in the second half, and Germany tied the score about ten minutes from the end. Neither team scored in a fairly conservative extra time, and the match went to a penalty shootout. Argentina and Germany had been the kings of penalty shootouts since the terrifying tiebreaker was introduced in 1982. Germany (technically West Germany at the time) won the first-ever shootout in the 1982 semifinal against France, and Argentina advanced via penalties twice in 1990 and once in 1998. Neither team had ever lost a World Cup penalty shootout. Something had to give in this one; that something was Argentina. The German goalkeeper Jens Lehmann saved two penalties and Germany won the shootout 4-2. Germany advanced through one historical opponent to face another.

It's natural that Italy and Germany have long been soccer rivals since they are the two most prolific European nations, each with three

World Cup championships to their credit. Italy defeated West Germany 3-1 to win the 1982 World Cup, but Germany lifted the trophy when the tournament was held on Italian soil in 1990. They also played in one of the all-time great matches in the history of the World Cup. The 4-3 extra-time victory for Italy in the 1970 World Cup semifinal is still widely regarded as the best World Cup game ever. Germany had never beaten Italy in any World Cup match, but historically speaking, even the Roman Empire eventually fell. Going into the current match, fans, observers, analysts, photographers, and reporters knew that if this match were half as entertaining as the historic encounter from 36 years earlier, the world would be in for a real treat.

As the players took the field in Dortmund, the stands were full of German flags waving excitedly. Germany had never lost a match in this city, and it was no coincidence that the schedulers had set up the bracket with Germany's potential semifinal match in this stadium. The atmosphere was electric; the two greatest European nations competing for a spot in the ultimate match. The Germans had the crowd advantage; the Italians had only each other, but that had been enough so far. The match began, and the dramatic festival was underway. No one knew it at the time, but everybody watching the game, in the stadium or around the world, was about to witness quite possibly the greatest soccer match ever played.

The Italian defense would have their hands full for the entire match with the most dangerous tandem of forwards in the entire tournament—Miroslav Klose and Lukas Podolski. Podolski scored both goals in Germany's 2-0 round of 16 victory over Sweden, and Klose scored the late equalizer to send the Argentina match into extra time. Klose also led all scorers in the tournament with five goals. Individually they were both excellent; together they were deadly. The action went back and forth from the start with each team creating some half chances. The first good chance came in the 16th minute, and it came for the Italians.

Francesco Totti saw his Roma teammate Simone Perrotta making a run down the left sideline towards the penalty box. Totti played a perfectly lofted ball right onto the foot of Perrotta, but his first touch was too hard, making the ball roll just a little bit too far in front of him; Lehmann reacted well and pounced on it. Perrotta had been an unheralded player during this World Cup. Entering the semifinal he was one of only three players on the team to have played every single minute of the tournament (the other two were Buffon and Cannavaro). Perrotta was a key reason for Italy's progress so far, and it would have been fitting for him to have finally scored a goal. The near miss also illustrated a key point for this match. Perrotta's bad touch was a minor mistake, but Lehmann made it seem worse than it was by his own terrific play. If any player was going to score in this match, it would have to be with a perfect play and a perfect shot; there would be no other way to beat the two best goalies in the world.

Germany had their first great chance in the 34th minute, and as anticipated, Klose was a key factor. The Germans were breaking quickly at the Italians with numbers up in a three-on-two situation. Klose was dribbling the ball centrally with Podolski running to his left and Bernd Schneider running on his right. The two defenders back for Italy were Cannavaro and Materazzi (back in the lineup after his one-game suspension). The defenders knew what they had to do; one of them had to stop the progress of the player with the ball, the other had to challenge the most dangerous scoring option, Podolski. Materazzi forced Klose to pass, and Cannavaro was closing on Podolski. Klose's best option was to incorporate Schneider. Klose laid off a perfect pass to Schneider, who collected the ball in the penalty area and fired a laser at the top portion of the goal. Buffon reacted well but the ball sailed over his outstretched fingertips. The German fans thought that they had taken the lead once the shot went past the 'keeper, but the ball flew over the crossbar by about three inches. The 65,000 spectators all gasped in unison (a few thousand were relieved), and the match remained scoreless. There were more opportunities through the first half and into the second half, but none as clear as the chances from Perrotta and Schneider.

In the 61st minute, Schneider created another golden opportunity. He played a nice ball to the feet of Podolski, who had his back to the goal near the corner of the six-yard box. Materazzi was covering him, but not for long. Podolski made a quick turn to create enough space to fire a clear shot at Buffon. As he had done so many times before, Buffon made a great save, using both fists to punch the ball away, and the rebound attempt was shot well over the goal.

In the 73rd minute, Juergen Klinsmann used his first substitution, bringing in Bastian Schweinsteiger to replace Tim Borowski. One minute later, Lippi used his first substitute, bringing on Alberto Gilardino to replace Luca Toni. Toni had put forth the usual maximum effort at the top of Italy's attack, but this game was played at such a frantic pace that he was tiring, and he couldn't make it two matches in a row with a goal. Germany continued to put on more pressure, and the Italians continued to defend with strength and discipline. Klinsmann used his second substitute in the 83rd minute, replacing Schneider with the speedy David Odonkor. Lippi held onto his final two substitutions, sensing that extra time was in the cards. He was right.

The first 90 minutes had finished without a goal, but the end-to-end action was enthralling. The first half was open with good chances for both teams, highlighted by good individual plays, mostly from the goalies. The second half was played a little bit more conservatively, with the home team more intent on getting the game's first goal. The match was everything one would expect and was more than anything one could have hoped for. For the neutral fan it must have been a completely entertaining 90 minutes; for German and Italian fans around the world it was nerve-wrenching torture. And now it would last for 30 additional minutes. At least.

At the start of the first extra time period, Lippi made his second substitution: Iaquinta in, Camoranesi out. Italy had been playing under a lot of pressure from Germany's attack during the latter part of the second half. Many coaches would've tried to solidify the defense by adding another defender or defensive midfielder. Lippi chose to insert another attacking player, trying to relieve some of the pressure on his defense by forcing the Germans to defend. It was a risky strategy, and the next few moments would show if it was a good one. Lippi's aggressive decision may have been spurred on by the threat of penalty kicks looming only half an hour away. Italy had been eliminated from the World Cup via the penalty shootout in 1990, 1994, and 1998. If the objective of avoiding penalties was foremost in the minds of the Italians, it would certainly explain the fantastic beginning to the extra time.

Less than 60 seconds into the first overtime period, Italy had a great chance. Gilardino, with his fresh legs, was chasing after German defender Christoph Metzelder, who was retreating near his own penalty area. Metzelder stumbled and Gilardino took the ball and made his way into the penalty area along the goal line. He cut the ball back around another defender and quickly shot the ball low along the ground. The shot rolled past Lehmann, who turned his head and watched the ball hit off the inside of the post and roll across the face of the open goal. No Italian player was there to tap it in, and Germany cleared the ball away. The 65,000 fans started breathing again. Moments later Italy earned a corner kick that was taken by Andrea Pirlo. The corner kick was deflected away by a German defender, but it went right to Zambrotta near the top of the penalty area. He took one touch to control the ball, and with his second touch he blasted a shot that soared past Lehmann and crashed off the crossbar. In less than two minutes Italy had hit the woodwork twice. The Italian players looked to the heavens in disbelief, while the Germans could only count their blessings and try to refocus.

As the first 15-minute extra time period was nearing conclusion, Lippi made his final substitution. Alessandro Del Piero was ready to enter the match, but instead of replacing Totti, as was the norm,

Perrotta was taken out of the game. Again, Lippi was risking a great deal taking out a midfielder and bringing in a striker. Perhaps Lippi was already preparing for the penalty shootout; perhaps he was so terrified of penalties that he would rather throw everything forward to try and avoid them and risk losing in overtime; perhaps he was just playing a hunch. In stoppage time of the first extra session, the Italians had their first defensive breakdown of the tournament. The German substitute Odonkor curled a cross into the penalty area, where Podolski was making a run to the near post. The cross was a perfect one, and somehow Podolski was wide open. The player who had caused the most anxious moments for the Italian defense was absolutely unmarked; he had plenty of time and space to head the ball into the goal, but he sent his powerful header wide of the target. Buffon was grateful he didn't need to make a save on the header, but he screamed at the top of his lungs at his defenders. The message was a desperate plea for his teammates to keep concentration—one more lapse like that and Italy would be playing for third place on Saturday. Buffon had already made plans to play on Sunday.

The second extra period began. Now there were only 15 minutes separating Italy from another shootout. The first half of the final 15 minutes was uneventful, except that every pass was so important that they all created incredible tension. A mistake at this stage would most likely spell defeat, which is why the teams made sure they didn't make any. With nine minutes remaining, Klinsmann made his final substitution, bringing in Oliver Neuville. Neuville had produced last-minute heroics off the bench in Germany's first-round meeting with Poland, when he scored the game-winning goal in the 91st minute. Klinsmann would have loved for him to repeat the feat against Italy, but with only nine minutes to play, it was more likely that the lineup change was in anticipation of the shootout; Neuville had converted his PK against Argentina.

One hundred twelve minutes into the match, as legs were growing weary and concentration was starting to slip, there was another great chance for Germany. Podolski found himself with room to shoot from inside the penalty area and slightly off to the right of Buffon. Cannavaro was closing quickly on Podolski, but he still had time to tee up a shot and unload a cannon at Buffon. Yet again, Buffon extended his arm and blocked the shot over the goal. It was an extremely critical and difficult save, and the grace and power with which Buffon did his job made clear that he was the greatest goalkeeper on Earth. It seemed like there was no way to score on Buffon. Germany had so many great chances to score, and no matter how good the shots, Buffon was always better. It was as if he knew where the shots were going before they were taken. Frustration was setting in for the Germans, and the penalty shootout looked unavoidable at this point.

With about three minutes to play in extra time, Buffon was ready to take a goal kick. One of the kids that retrieve the balls had tossed one out to Buffon for the goal kick, but instead of using that one Buffon went near the corner flag to collect the ball that had just recently gone out of play. The angry German fans whistled derisively, seeing this gesture as a clear time-wasting act from Buffon. The fans wanted their team to have one last chance to win in regulation, and Buffon was intentionally trying to delay the restart and get to penalties. About 20 wasted seconds later, Buffon finally blasted the goal kick high in the air across midfield towards the right sideline.

The ball went towards Iaquinta, who did a nice job to control it with his chest, but as he did so, Schweinsteiger knocked the ball away from behind him. Fortunately for the Italians, the ball sailed to Gennaro Gattuso, who kept possession for Italy and passed it backwards into his own half for Zambrotta. Zambrotta played a long ball down the sideline for Iaquinta, who volleyed the ball for Gilardino, who sent the ball to Pirlo. As Pirlo was controlling the ball, the German defender in pursuit slipped, allowing Pirlo to carry the ball forward into the attacking third. The German defenders were retreating; making sure that Pirlo couldn't send a through ball to one of the strikers. Without a good passing angle, Pirlo took a shot from long range. The left-footed shot was a powerful one, moving towards the upper corner. Lehmann was well positioned (of course) and blocked the shot out of bounds for a corner. Pirlo held his head in his hands, feeling perhaps that with less than two minutes left, the final chance for Italy to win before the shootout had just been saved. Italy still had the corner kick, and this would surely be the last chance, now less than 90 seconds from the final whistle. The tall defender Fabio Grosso had come forward for the corner kick.

Del Piero sent the curving corner into the penalty area, and it was deflected low out of the box. Pirlo stood just outside the penalty area. The hard clearance was right at Pirlo, who used good skills to control the ball. He was only 18 yards away from the goal, but with all of the German defenders clogging up the box, he couldn't find enough space to shoot. As he dribbled laterally to the right along the top of the box there was a sea of white shirts seemingly cutting off every angle. Then out of the corner of his eye, Pirlo saw a sliver of space to send the ball to a teammate. Pirlo's pass was a perfect one for Grosso, who turned a one-time shot towards the German goal. Lehman dove for it at full stretch, but it was beyond his reach. The left-footed shot appeared to be going wide, but there was so much spin on the ball that it curled itself into the goal right against the post. Italy went in front 1-0.

It was pandemonium for the Italians. The only way to beat the goalkeepers today was with a perfect shot, and if Grosso took that same shot one million times, he could not have hit one any better.

* * * *

In the 1982 World Cup final in Madrid, Italy played against West Germany. Italy was ahead 1-0 nearing the 70-minute mark. The Italian sweeper Gaetano Scirea made an aggressive foray into the attacking third and set up what would become the game-winning goal. The player who scored the goal for Italy was Marco Tardelli. After the critical goal, Tardelli ran down the field, screaming and pumping both his fists in front of him. The vision of Tardelli's celebratory display is one that is often shown during the World Cup. Anyone who has ever scene the video clip of Tardelli knows the exact image; in fact most people recognize the highlight without even knowing who the player is. Tardelli seems to be having an out-of-body experience, and his face is an impossible blend of agony, fury, and euphoria that somehow expresses his ecstasy. Italians around the world understand the significance of Tardelli's moment forever frozen in time, and as Grosso started running towards the sideline in celebration, the tears were welling in his eyes; he was shaking his head and waving his right index finger—it was a truly *Tardellian* moment.

His head was shaking as he was wagging his finger, apparently saying "No" about something. Who knows what Grosso was saying no about—no penalty shootout; no, we're not going to lose; no, we're not done yet; no celebrating for the 65,000 fans in Dortmund. Whatever the message from Grosso, there were millions of individuals back home in Italy screaming "Yes."

As Grosso ran in triumph towards the sideline, Zambrotta tackled him. Del Piero soon dove on top of the two of them, and the next player who leapt on top of the pile was Buffon, who had run about 80 yards to be a part of the chaos. On the Italian bench the coaching staff was going berserk as well, all except Lippi. He was smiling widely as he accepted a warm embrace from Gattuso, but as Gattuso made his way back to the field, Lippi had an important message for him, something along the lines of, "We still have to survive 90 more seconds."

A few yards away to Lippi's right, Juergen Klinsmann was applauding his team trying to keep their hopes up. Germany had a few seconds left; maybe they could duplicate Italy's miracle. After the kick-off, the Germans ran forward at full speed into the attacking third. Odonkor whipped in a cross towards the near post, which was cleared by a diving header from Cannavaro. The clearance rolled to Michael Ballack, the German leader and team captain. He had a good look at the goal, but his shot was high and wide.

Buffon's ensuing goal kick was controlled near midfield by Germany. As they quickly made their way into the attacking third down the left sideline, they sent another hopeful ball into the box. Cannavaro was there again; almost single-handedly ensuring that Germany was not going to tie the match. This time Cannavaro headed the ball high into the air and about 30 yards away from the goal. The ball was coming down slowly and none of his teammates were moving towards it, so Cannavaro went after it himself. Podolski tried to control the ball with his chest, but he was quickly overwhelmed by the Italian captain who knocked the ball away, controlled it, and moved forward in possession. Near the center circle his momentum carried him into his teammate Totti. The two bumped into each other, Totti kept the ball, and Cannavaro retreated to his central defensive position. Totti sent a long through ball on the ground to Gilardino, who had a lot of space since so many Germans had gone forward. Gilardino was one-on-one near the top of the box when he heard a teammate calling for the ball. Alessandro Del Piero had run for about 85 yards to try and get involved in the counterattack. Gilardino rolled the ball into the path of Del Piero, who entered the box and one-timed the ball past Lehmann into the upper corner of the goal. Italy moved in front 2-0 and into the World Cup final. For the second match of the tournament, an Italian goal was the final kick of the match.

The Italians had done it again. Fabio Grosso, the man who earned the penalty kick in the dying seconds against Australia, was a national hero for the second time in eight days. Alex Del Piero, who had been reduced to a reserve for nearly the entire tournament, came through with a critical goal at the most opportune moment. Italy remained undefeated against Germany in World Cup history, and again the Italians had come away with a momentous victory in a match that will rank as one of the greatest ever. The success of the team continued to be based on the concept of team, as two new players put their names on the score sheet, bringing the grand total to ten different players who scored a goal in this tournament.

Back in Italy, the people were going wild. It was more than just the fact that the team was back in the final; it was the way in which they got there. Seconds away from the penalty shootout that had eliminated Italy from three out of the last four World Cups, they scored a magnificent goal that sent a wave of glorious bedlam through Italians everywhere. All Italian fans will always remember exactly where they were when Pirlo somehow found the space to slide a pass to Grosso. With one beautiful left-footed curling shot, Fabio Grosso put Italy into the World Cup final, put his entire nation into a state of jubilation, and put himself into Italian stardom. The ball was only in contact with his foot for a millisecond, but that instant will be remembered forever.

Pirlo, Grosso, and Del Piero were the clear heroes of the final moments, and they deserve all of the recognition that they receive for their timely displays of brilliance. The efforts of these three players would not have been possible however if it hadn't been for two players who had already left their marks on the match from the other end of the stadium. Fabio Cannavaro and Gianluigi Buffon perfectly orchestrated one of the greatest defensive units ever assembled.

It's easy to see the excellence of Buffon. His positioning, composure, skill, and athleticism are as obvious as they are remarkable. Every time Buffon stretches to make a save, dives on a loose ball, or punches away a cross, everybody notices, and rightly so.

Cannavaro's abilities are much more subtle, but equally important. Many times Cannavaro will snuff out an attack before it even has a chance to produce a shot. Cannavaro can be far away from the ball, but his presence on the field can change the decision making of his opponents. Players choose to pass the ball backwards to a teammate since Cannavaro can effortlessly take away a pass intended for a striker. There is no player on the planet that understands and anticipates the movements of opposing attacking players like Fabio Cannavaro. Throughout the tournament he had been the best defender, and quite possibly the best overall player. Only one more match was keeping the world's greatest goalie and the world's greatest defender from the world's greatest prize.

18

Italy 2–Germany 0

Major League Soccer has a history of playing games on the Fourth of July, regardless of what day of the week it is. It seems like specifically in the Midwest these matches are extremely popular. Families make a holiday out of these games and the stadiums have fireworks at the conclusion of the matches. D.C. United was scheduled to play in Dallas on July 4. In my opinion, MLS made a big mistake in scheduling matches on that afternoon, since it was also the semifinal of the World Cup, and potentially it could have been a match involving Team U.S.A. If that scenario had played out, very few American soccer fans would've been concentrating on FC Dallas or D.C. United or any other MLS franchise. At any rate, Team U.S.A. had long since been eliminated from the World Cup, and the MLS fans could enjoy both matches one after the other. For the MLS game announcers it wouldn't be so easy.

There was enough time for the Italy–Germany match to end before I had to begin the pre-production work for the United match. But, of course, once the game went into overtime I was living on borrowed time before having to focus on the MLS game. I am very grateful to my producer Rich Wolff who was patient and gracious in allowing me to watch the entire overtime, thus delaying his production schedule and putting him under the gun. I don't know what he would've done if the match had gone to penalties. I was in the media lunchroom in Pizza Hut Park watching the overtime with my colleagues Doug Hicks and Garth Lagerwey. When Grosso scored I ran to the flat screen TV (I was only standing about six feet away) pumping my fists and screaming "Come on!" I usually try to play it cool when I'm working, but there wasn't much chance this time. Then moments later when Gilardino was moving towards the top of the box, my friend Doug said, "Dribble to the corner." I said, "No way, go score again." Del Piero followed my advice, and as soon as the ball hit the net I ran down the hall to our broadcast booth to begin focusing on the United game.

After the match (which United won 1-0 on a beautiful goal from Christian Gomez) we went back to the hotel before a bunch of us went out to dinner. On our way back out to dinner the team had arrived from the stadium. Christian Gomez came up to me and said something like, "How about that Italy game?" I told him I couldn't breathe I was so excited. I know he wasn't happy about Italy, but I thought it was nice that he at least seemed happy for me. When we made it to the restaurant there were TV's all over, and the highlights from the Germany game seemed to come on about every 15 minutes or so. I watched them all and cheered for Grosso's goal every time. When I finally made it back to the hotel, I got a call from Nori telling me that the match was being replayed on TV. She called me while I was in the lobby getting ready to get on the elevator and she said that the game was in the 10th minute of the second overtime. It was another instance of perfect timing that day. I didn't change my pace at all, and as I opened the door to my room and turned on the TV, Germany had just kicked the ball out of play for Buffon's final goal kick.

It was an exciting and anxious next few days. All my family could talk about was the Italy game. I told my father that I thought even if it had gone to penalties Italy probably would have won. It seemed like everybody got the sense that on that day in Dortmund, Italy was not going to be denied. It's also an easy thing to agree with when there is no way to disprove it. So, I arrived home from Dallas on Wednesday, July 5. That afternoon, France defeated Portugal to earn their place in the final match. Three days later I had to go back on the road to Columbus for a match on Saturday July 8. This was the day of the World Cup third place match in which Germany beat Portugal 3-1. United won 1-0 and some colleagues and I gathered for another celebratory dinner. At dinner that night I was really nervous. I was enjoying the company of my friends, but at the same time I was thinking about Zidane, Henry, and Trezeguet, the most dangerous French players. I was happy to stay out late, since I didn't think I'd be able to sleep anyway. I finally made it back to my room, just a few hours from when my wake-up call was scheduled. It was an early flight back home.

It's funny how often things go horribly wrong. There are so many crazy things that happen that make me think to myself, "If I saw this happen in a movie I would think it was totally absurd!" Yet it was one of these moments that started my day on July 9, 2006. I was still in Columbus, Ohio. It was the morning after the D.C. United game. That morning I was going to the airport to catch a flight back home to D.C. to watch the most important sporting event of my life. I was awake earlier than necessary, probably due to my mounting anxiety. I was meeting my colleague, Frank Hanrahan, in the lobby to go to the airport, but since I had arrived at our meeting point about 15 minutes early I decided to go to the rental car and load my suitcase. The car had a flat tire. My emotions quickly went from anxiety to total panic. I actually felt myself start sweating immediately. The only good news was that Frank wasn't with me so I had a few minutes to melt down in private. I quickly called the car rental company to tell them my plan to leave the car in the hotel parking lot so they could come tow it back to their office, while I would take a taxi to the airport.

There was another problem. The car rental location in Columbus wasn't open yet, so I had to talk to the national headquarters' 24-hour people. It was a big mess, but I soon realized that I wasn't going to miss my flight and that the rental company would just have to agree to my terms. Their car was waiting for them in the garage, and I had much more important things to worry about. So we made our flight with no additional delays, and I made it home in plenty of time to make it to my parents' house to watch the game.

Most of that day leading up to the game was a blur. The flat tire was memorable, but there's really only one other thing that sticks out in my mind about that morning. While I was driving home from the airport I remembered that it was the birthday of one of United's players, Alecko Eskandarian. One year earlier, United played on his birthday, and when I wished him happy birthday outside the locker room he got a big smile on his face and said, "You remembered my birthday!" I was surprised at how surprised he looked, and since it seemed to cheer him up last year I thought I'd call him this year. Secretly I was hoping he wouldn't answer. He didn't answer; I left a message wishing him a happy birthday and felt like I had done everything in my power to have the positive karma needed for an Italian victory. To be honest I didn't feel like I needed luck—I *knew* we were going to win.

Nervous energy was oozing in my parents' house like fresh mozzarella when I arrived for the game. I was wearing my Christmas gift from Lorenzo, and everybody talked and joked to try and help everybody else relax. It didn't work. Up until this point in the tournament, we had watched the games with people who were less intense about their feelings for the Italian national team. Those are the kind of people who like soccer, and support Italy, but won't think about the game every day for the next eight months if Italy loses. It's not a problem that we had been watching games with them before, but this game was too special to risk any distractions, even minor ones. There were no "non-believers" in the house today. The crowd was an intimate one, just the immediate family—Mom, Pop, Meg, Lorenzo, Pep, Kristen, Brigid, Alex, Nori, Mikey, Elizabeth, Johnny, Emily— and Laura and Anna. Technically, my wife and the wife or girlfriends of my brothers don't take it as seriously as we do, but they provide essential moral support. I was happy the Italian girls were there, too;

it was a nice connection to the branch of the family from Castellamare. I felt like a lot of the suffering in World Cups past was intrinsically linked to those cousins, and now we could share the ultimate success with them as well. Okay, after the pomp and circumstance were finally over, it was time to start the match. Somehow we all sort of have normal positions in the room when we watch important games. Pop has a recliner that he sits in. Mikey sits in a big leather chair with ottoman in the corner of the room. Nori sits on the couch across the room from Mikey, guests and others usually take the love seat. Pep likes to pace, so he hangs out in the kitchen and watches the TV across the bar that separates the two rooms. As usual in a crowded family room, I stood behind Pop's chair.

19

The Final—July 9
Italy vs. France—Berlin

The Italian fans had no reason to be nervous during the match versus Germany; it was a virtual certainty that Italy would be in the finals. Italy makes it to the World Cup championship match every 12 years. It's as indisputable as a scientific conclusion of Galileo. In 1970, Italy made it to the finals (after the classic match versus West Germany) and lost to Brazil. In 1982, Italy won the World Cup in Spain behind one of the greatest goal poachers of all-time, Paolo Rossi. In 1994, Italy lost to Brazil in the finals again, this time on a penalty shootout in Los Angeles, California. Now in 2006 they had made it back to the ultimate game in sports just as nature expected.

The Italy vs. Germany semifinal was played on Tuesday; then the following day, as many Italian fans were just returning home from partying in the piazzas the other semifinal took place between France and Portugal. This semifinal was less exhilarating than its counterpart from 24 hours earlier. France was given a penalty kick in the first half that was converted by Zinedine Zidane. Portugal did everything they could think of to try and find the equalizer, but the elusive goal never materialized. Most of the neutral fans in that match were pleased with France's 1-0 victory—firstly because the Portuguese had resorted to bad tactics and a lot of diving, which is the quickest way to earn enemies in a world soccer audience. The other reason that the public was happy to see France in the final was because it would give Zinedine Zidane one last performance on the greatest stage in sports. Zidane had been a hero to millions for a generation, and what better way to cement his place in history than with another World Cup trophy. It had been a difficult road for France to reach the final.

France was in a relatively easy foursome during group play. Group G consisted of France, Switzerland, the Republic of Korea, and Togo. It seemed like France could play using only their left feet and still advance. But after they tied their first match 0-0 with Switzerland and allowed a late equalizing goal against Korea, they entered their final match in absolute need of a win. At that point the French were in dire straits. They hadn't won a match since the 1998 World Cup final. They were eliminated after three games in Korea/Japan, and they had two ties so far in this tournament. What made matters worse for France was that they had to play the group-phase finale without Zidane, who had collected a yellow card in each of the first two matches and earned a suspension for what could have been France's last game of the tournament.

Patrick Vieira filled in admirably in Zidane's absence, scoring a goal and setting up another to ensure that France got the two goals necessary to advance versus Togo. The team of aging greats backed their way into the second round and was likely to get knocked out of the tournament by a Spanish side that had been firing on all cylinders since their opening match, a 4-0 victory. But in their match versus Spain, Zidane was rejuvenated, and his teammates followed his example. Spain took an early advantage on a penalty kick, but then an excellent individual effort from one of the rare French youngsters, Frank Ribery, tied the match at 1-1 before halftime. From that point the game was even with good chances for both teams, but after losing their early lead the Spaniards appeared disheartened. Seven minutes away from full time Spain committed a foul in the attacking third, giving Zidane a late opportunity to work his magic. His free kick was deflected by a Spanish defender and went towards Vieira, who elevated well and headed the ball off the leg of another Spanish defender and into the goal. Two cruel deflections meant Spain was only a few minutes from elimination. They quickly refocused but couldn't tie the match, and Zidane added the late exclamation point with a goal in stoppage time.

The quarterfinal was the setting for the rematch of the last two World Cup champions, France and Brazil. The Brazilians were still the favorite to advance, but in this game they seemed almost uninterested. The game remained scoreless and fairly uneventful until Zidane had another free kick. This time from the opposite side of the field he sent a ball across the box to Thierry Henry, who smashed a volley from close range that put France in front. The atrocious marking on that play represented the lethargic attitude of the Brazilians throughout the tournament. Despite scoring goals in bunches their play was not what the world had expected, and they were rightly eliminated in the quarterfinals. France ended the run of the defending champions and then got past Portugal to take on the Italians.

One of the most enjoyable elements of Germany 2006 was the plethora of classic matchups: Argentina vs. Holland, Mexico vs. Argentina, England vs. Portugal, Spain vs. France, Germany vs. Argentina, France vs. Brazil, Germany vs. Italy, and now Italy vs. France. It was very fitting that the culmination of the fabulous tournament would be decided between two of the world powers. These teams had previously met four times in the World Cup. In their first meeting, Italy won in the 1938 quarterfinals when the tournament was played in France, but France avenged that home defeat in their most recent World Cup meeting in 1998, knocking Italy out in a quarterfinal penalty shootout. Between those meetings, Italy beat France in group play in 1978, and France eliminated Italy in the round of 16 in 1986. Their most recent head-to-head confrontation, which was not from a World Cup, was still on the minds of fans from both sides.

In the 2000 European Cup, these teams met in the final. Italy pulled in front with about 20 minutes left, but France threw everybody forward for the remainder of the game and tied the game in the final 30 seconds of stoppage time to send the match into overtime. In overtime, David Trezeguet scored the golden goal to win the tournament. For Italian players and fans that defeat was one of the most painful. Italy was seconds away from lifting the trophy and instead of a championship victory they were left with a soul-shattering defeat. That match was played six years earlier, but there were several key players involved again. As the World Cup final began, the Euro final started to temporarily fade from memory, but the emotional baggage from that famous match would resurface several times during this even more momentous game.

Some World Cup finals start off slowly with both teams taking their time and allowing the players to lose the nervous energy from playing in the biggest match in the world. This final was not one of them. Only six minutes into the match, France was on the attack as Florent Malouda went running into the penalty area. Malouda went down as he was chasing the ball, and the Argentinean referee Horacio Elizondo awarded a penalty kick. Materazzi was in disbelief. The television replays show that there was minimal contact between Materazzi's leg and the foot of Malouda, and the decision of the referee would certainly change the complexion of the game. Gianluigi Buffon had saved every shot taken by the opponents the entire tournament, but he had yet to face one from the penalty spot. Naturally, Zinedine Zidane stepped up to the ball. Only six minutes into the game, and the stage was already set for Zidane to become the hero in his last professional game ever. Elizondo blew his whistle, Zidane approached and struck the ball, and Buffon dove to his right.

Usually, players who take penalties believe that if they hit the ball properly, the goalie cannot save it. Many also believe that the harder the ball is hit, the less likely the goalie is to make a save, even if he guesses correctly and dives the right way. Still others, who trust their ability to read their opponents, will wait until the goalie makes a move and then place their shot accordingly. Then there are players, oozing with self-confidence sprinkled with arrogance, who assume the goalie will dive to one side or the other in anticipation of the shot. When these smug players are convinced the goalkeeper will move before the shot and not react to the shot, they intentionally chip the ball very softly into the air so that it floats gently into the net. If it works for the shooter the goal is twice as nice, you score the goal and you show off your personal fortitude at the same time. If somehow the kicker misses or has his chip shot saved, he is forever a goat, knowing full well that there is no excuse for taking such a serious moment so lightly.

For Zidane to try a chip shot in the World Cup championship match was audacious bordering on lunacy. The ball floated high in the air toward the goal, far from Buffon, who already dove to the ground. The ball hit the crossbar, fell to the ground and bounced out of the goal. The Italian players raced to clear it away, but the officials indicated that the ball had gone fully across the line before bouncing out and was therefore a goal. The referee's decision on the foul leading to the penalty was debatable; the decision about whether the ball crossed the line was not. The television replays clearly confirmed that the ball was fully across the line, and France was in front 1-0.

Italy had played 577 minutes in the tournament up to this point, and for the first time they were trailing an opponent. It was the first goal that Buffon had allowed to an opposing player this World Cup. Italy had been meeting difficult challenges head-on throughout the World Cup, both on and off the field, and now in the most important match it was the most difficult challenge. Historically, there was good news and bad news for Italy. The bad news was that it had been 32 years since a team allowed the first goal in the final and came back to win. The good news was that the last time it did occur, it happened in Germany. For the Italians, their current situation was too important for historical analysis.

Things nearly went from bad to dismal a few moments later, when Materazzi's header almost went past Buffon for another goal. The Italian defense was astoundingly beginning to falter. The Italians needed to refocus and settle down, and they needed to do it quickly. The game regained some flow, and as is often the case, the team playing from behind began to apply more pressure. In the 19th minute the pressure earned them a corner kick. Mauro Camoranesi was one-on-one near the corner flag and did very well to win a corner kick by knocking the ball off a defender. Camoranesi was then preparing to take the kick when Andrea Pirlo indicated that he wanted to take it. Looking back, it's a good thing for the Italians that Pirlo didn't let Camoranesi take the kick. Pirlo had been the guiding force to the offense since the tournament began. Throughout Italy's run to the final he had been successful in earning Italy a lead; this time he needed to help them equalize. Pirlo curled the corner kick into the penalty area and Marco Materazzi rose above the French defenders and smashed the header past the French goalie Fabian Barthez to tie the score 1-1.

* * * *

What an emotional roller coaster the World Cup had been for Materazzi. He began the tournament on the bench as a clear backup to Alessandro Nesta. Nesta's injury allowed Materazzi an opportunity to take the field, and Materazzi made the most of it by scoring against Czech Republic. He knew that he would remain in the starting lineup due to Nesta's injury but then received a red card versus Australia. After the unforgettable victory over Germany in the semifinal he began the most important game of his life by giving up a penalty kick, and then only 12 minutes later he scored the most important goal he would ever score. There were more emotional surges still to come for Materazzi.

The goal from Italy gave them an emotional boost, and also marked the first time since 1986 that both teams had scored a goal in the World Cup final. Italy tried to ride the momentum from their first goal into a second. They nearly did. Once again, a corner kick provided the needed opportunity. Pirlo crossed into the box again, and in a play nearly identical to Materazzi's goal, Luca Toni blasted a header past Barthez. This time however the ball hit the crossbar and sailed out of play. Toni stood on the field with his face in his hands, in utter disbelief that he couldn't put his team in front. Luck had not been with Toni during this tournament; this shot was the second time he hit the crossbar. Italy finished the half as the more aggressive team, but the score was 1-1 at halftime.

In the second half the tide shifted. Suddenly France looked poised to move in front once again, led by Thierry Henry. His speed and skills were beginning to cause problems for the Italian defense, but Buffon, Cannavaro, and company kept all of his attempts in check. In the 53rd minute, Malouda streaked into the penalty box again, and for the second time in the match he went down in a heap. This time the referee waved for him to get up, although this challenge from Gianluca Zambrotta looked much worse than the foul that created the penalty in the first half. Three minutes later, France faced another disappointment as Patrick Vieira was forced to leave the game with a leg injury. Vieira had been one of the best players in the entire tournament, doing whatever was necessary for the French. Italy gained a little more confidence seeing that they would no longer have to worry about Vieira scoring or making a key defensive play.

Lippi made a double substitution. He removed Francesco Totti and Simone Perrotta in exchange for Vincenzo Iaquinta and Daniele De Rossi. Totti was Italy's best penalty taker, and now if the match went all the way to a shootout, another player would be placed into the fire. Iaquinta had come on as a substitute in four previous matches, and was involved in the late heroics versus Germany. Using De Rossi was a surprise decision from Lippi. De Rossi hadn't played since his red card against the United States. In fact, he had been suspended for the four matches since then. When he learned of his extended suspension, De Rossi must have thought that his tournament was over, but here he was entering the World Cup final with the score tied. De Rossi was a defensive center midfielder, so when he replaced Totti, Pirlo slid a little farther forward, and De Rossi played closer to Gennaro Gattuso. Lippi had created a midfield chock-full of grit, energy, and determination—the perfect way to combat the skill, patience, and creativity of France's midfield.

Just past the hour mark of the match Pirlo had another free kick for the Italians. Once again he sent the ball into the penalty area trying to pick out the excellent target of Luca Toni. This time they connected perfectly, Toni headed the ball into the goal and the Italians were celebrating again. It was a much-abbreviated celebration as the assistant referee had raised his flag for offsides. The joy quickly turned into frustration, and the match remained tied. Pirlo was involved again in the 78th minute, this time sending a swerving free kick directly at goal. The shot curved over the wall and zipped mere inches wide of the post. Four minutes from overtime, Lippi used his final substitution, bringing in Alessandro Del Piero to replace Camoranesi. Del Piero struck in the semifinal seconds before the final whistle; he would have a chance to do the same again. The match reached the end of regulation with the sides still deadlocked at one. Now, just like their last head-to-head meeting, the match would go into extra time.

Ten minutes into the first overtime session, Ribery had the best opportunity for France. He found some space at the top of the penalty area after a give and go with Malouda and sent a powerful shot skidding on the grass. Buffon dove for it, but it was out of his reach and finished just wide of the post. That was the last shot for Ribery, literally, as he was subbed out of the game after that play. Ribery played an excellent game and an excellent tournament, clearly establishing himself as one of the top young players in the world. Coming in to replace Ribery was David Trezeguet. Trezeguet had been used sparingly throughout the tournament, but the Italians knew the danger that he would create. Trezeguet made his living in Italy playing for Juventus, so his teammates and his opponents in Serie A would know what to expect from Trezeguet; it was just a matter of if they could stop it. Scoring late goals has always been what Trezeguet enjoys most.

In the final moments of the first extra time period came one of the most memorable plays of the World Cup. Zidane played a ball to the right sideline for the overlapping defender Willy Sagnol. Sagnol then sent a perfect return cross to Zidane, who was racing through the penalty area. Zidane elevated, connected with the ball, and snapped a header on target.

* * * *

Eight years earlier during the 1998 World Cup final, Zinedine Zidane became a national and world hero when he scored two goals in the first half to give the host nation a 2-0 lead over the defending champions, Brazil. Both goals were crosses that Zidane powerfully headed home. France won the game 3-0 to claim their first and only World Cup. Zidane was at the top of the world, he had played his best game on the biggest stage, and he would be considered one of the all-time greats. Now, he was about to put his team in front in overtime in the World Cup final and claim his nation's second World Cup trophy.

The header was flying towards the goal, sure to go in right beneath the crossbar. Just then the hand of Gianluigi Buffon knocked the ball away over the top of the bar. Zidane looked around in disbelief. Everything was set up perfectly for the French: an excellent cross, a great run, and a powerful header on target from close range. Zidane must have already been celebrating the go-ahead goal in his mind when the reflexes of Buffon gave him a cold dose of reality. This moment was the decisive one of the match. This play symbolized everything that both teams had worked for during the preceding month since the opening game of the World Cup.

France had been a patient team, seemingly just slightly above average. They went for long periods without being impressive, but when the moment was right they had made every critical play necessary. France had a very competent supporting cast, but the keystone that held all the other blocks together was Zidane, and the team could only go as far as he could take them. That's why when Zidane rose for the header, the French players and fans knew that he would score. There could not be a more appropriate ending than the late game-winning goal from Zidane—on a header, just like his World Cup winning goal from 1998.

Italy had been battling adversity since before the tournament even began. There were more distractions for the Italians than for any of the 32 teams in the tournament. In spite of the potential for disaster, in spite of the impending doom, in spite of the rest of the world just waiting for them to lose, the Italians had individually and collectively always risen to the occasion. There was no clearer example of impending doom at any point for the Italians than Zidane's header. The Italians had made every critical play necessary throughout the tournament, and their leader, Buffon, was not about to become the one player who failed on his responsibility to his teammates. He knocked the ball away and the score stayed 1-1.

The save was awe inspiring, easily the best save of the game—and of the tournament—and possibly of any World Cup final match. The timing, reflexes, and reaction were all absolutely perfect; anything less would have meant a sure goal. Buffon showed the reflexes of a ninja, the athleticism of a decathlete, and the coordination of a trapeze artist. Goalkeepers don't often show their emotion during a game when they make a good play; they tend to leave the flamboyance for the goal scorers. But after this save from Buffon he was clearly energized. He showed exuberance that he normally keeps inside, as perhaps he knew that from that point Italy was not to be denied.

The first extra time period ended goalless and the world was now 15 minutes from a penalty shootout. Thierry Henry was substituted out of the match in the 107th minute. Henry had been France's most dangerous player, and it might have been a relief for the Italian defense to see him going off if it had been a different player who was entering in his place. Sylvain Wiltord entered the game as France's final substitute, and each player off the bench for France might as well have been a ghost from six years earlier. Wiltord was the player who scored the goal seconds away from the final whistle to steal the victory from Italy in Euro 2000. It didn't seem like the Italians would ever be able to get past that game.

The extra session wound slowly towards its conclusion when the two goal scorers became involved in an altercation that changed history. France had an opportunity in the attacking third that was dealt with by the Italian defense. As the players were moving back downfield, Zidane and Materazzi exchanged words. Zidane distanced himself from Materazzi, and then quickly turned around and drove his head directly into Materazzi's chest sending him to the ground. A few moments later the referee brought play to a halt, consulted with his assistant referee, and showed Zidane a red card for his savage attack. In a totally inexplicable turn of events, Zidane's wondrous career ended with a cowardly act of violence. Zidane, who had been the most obvious reason for France's run to the final, the man who had at times carried his teammates and his nation on his shoulders, the man who had inspired an entire team to play at their best, had thrown it all away with an unnecessary cheap shot. Zidane's intent was to hurt or injure Materazzi, but instead he inflicted great pain on all the players, coaches, and fans that had ever supported him.

The match continued without any more scoring. Materazzi's goal in the 19th minute was the last tally of the match, and now, once the shock of Zidane's exit had temporarily passed, the significance of the game came into focus. The World Cup, the most coveted trophy in all of sports, was going to be decided by penalties. The weight of the world falls on the shoulders of the players involved, and for the Italians, that weight had always been unbearable.

In 1990, in a World Cup semifinal match played in Naples, Italy experienced their first penalty shootout. Roberto Baggio, Franco Baresi, and Luigi DiAgostini all converted their kicks, before Roberto

Donadoni's and Aldo Serena's were both saved. Losing at home in front of a crowd full of supporters might have been the most disappointing way to lose a penalty shootout, except for the following World Cup. The final match of the 1994 World Cup was the first championship to be decided on penalties. Franco Baresi missed the first kick in that shootout, before Demetrio Albertini and Alberigo Evani scored. Daniele Massaro's attempt was saved, setting the stage for Roberto Baggio, who missed the final kick, giving Brazil their fourth World Cup. In 1998 Italy and France met in a World Cup quarterfinal penalty shootout. In that shootout, Roberto Baggio scored, Demetrio Albertini missed, Alessandro Costacurta and Christian Vieri scored, and the final kick from Luigi Di Biaggio hit the crossbar. The history was bleak. The only bit of good news was that in the semifinal of the 2000 European Cup, Italy did defeat Holland in a penalty shootout.

The team captains returned to the center circle for another coin toss, and it was decided that Italy would kick first. As the goalies walked to take their positions, Buffon and Barthez shared an embrace and a smile. It was certainly not gamesmanship, just an attempt to try and calm the nerves, and a true tribute to the motto of this World Cup, *A Time to Make Friends*. With the niceties over, it was time for the first kick. No one was smiling now.

Andrea Pirlo was the first player to take a kick. As he set up the ball and waited for the referee's whistle, he forced down a swallow and then kept his mouth closed, possibly trying to keep himself from throwing up. Pirlo had been Italy's most consistent attacking player throughout the tournament. He was a candidate for the Golden Ball (most valuable player of the World Cup), and he was a quiet leader for the team. He scored the first goal of the tournament for Italy, assisted on the game-winning goal in the final seconds of the semifinal, and collected another assist on the equalizing goal in this final. He had one more job to do. The whistle went and Pirlo shot. Barthez dove to his right; the shot went high and central, right down the middle. Italy started well 1-0.

First up for France was Wiltord. He had only played about 15 minutes in this game, so he didn't need to worry about tired legs like most of the players. The whistle from the ref was heard and Wiltord scored, sending Buffon the wrong way. 1-1 after one kick apiece.

Round two began with Materazzi moving to take his kick. The crowd was whistling very loudly as he walked to the penalty spot. The fans in the stadium were not privy to the television replay that showed Zidane's head butt, so they assumed that Materazzi had taken a dive. The rude reception from the fans was the last thing on Materazzi's mind. For Materazzi, the entire tournament had been a terrible mix of joys and sorrows. He was currently on an upswing, since he was a hero for scoring Italy's only goal, but his emotions had gone back and forth so quickly so many times. It was time to put two joyous moments back-to-back. Materazzi was ready, the whistle blew, and he calmly slotted the ball into the lower left corner, just a few inches beyond the outstretched hand of Barthez. 2-1 in favor of Italy with France's second kick coming up.

David Trezeguet was the man to take kick number two for France. Once again it was a substitute for France who would try the kick; Italy's first two takers had played the full two hours. Trezeguet was ready, facing his Juventus teammate Buffon. The whistle blew and Trezeguet struck, Buffon went down to his left, and the ball went high to the right. Too high. The ball banged off the bottom of the crossbar, hit the ground near the goal line, and bounced away from the goal. Trezeguet looked at the referees, hoping that maybe his kick snuck across the line as Zidane's penalty did all the way back in the 7th minute. The referees confirmed that the ball didn't cross the line, and Italy led 2-1 after two complete rounds.

Round three for Italy, and Daniele De Rossi was taking the long, lonely walk from midfield to the penalty spot. De Rossi could not have possibly anticipated being in this situation. His foolish play that earned him a red card was very likely to be his last act of the tournament. Somehow he persevered and was now trying to make up for his mistake by converting this penalty. All would be forgiven if he scored here. The pressure in these situations is beyond description, even for the most experienced players. De Rossi was the youngest player on either roster. The whistle from the ref and De Rossi blasted a shot into the upper left corner. The shot was the best so far, unstoppable. Italy was in front 3-1 with France's third attempt coming up.

Eric Abidal stepped up next for France. This was the first player for France who had to worry about fatigue, having played the entire match. A miss here would give Italy a huge lead. Abidal scored easily, as Buffon dove the wrong way. Still the narrowest of leads for Italy 3-2.

The fourth round of a penalty shootout always seems to be the most important. Many times the final outcome is determined in the fourth round, and even if it's not decisive, missing the fourth kick almost always spells defeat, as it did for Italy in 1990 and in 1994. Coaches often place their best PK takers in that position, and that's what Lippi did as he assigned Alex Del Piero to the fourth kick. Del Piero had not been as involved as he would have liked during the tournament, coming off the bench for Italy. He scored the insurance goal against Germany, and now he had his chance to leave his mark on the final. In the Euro 2000 final versus France, Del Piero had two clear chances to give Italy a two-goal lead and wrap up that championship. He failed to capitalize on those chances and left the door open for France's comeback. Del Piero had a chance to wipe that memory clean and maybe put France away now. Whistle. Shot. Goal. Italy had made their first four kicks to lead the shootout 4-2, and now it was do or die for France.

As Willy Sagnol stepped to the ball for France's fourth kick, Buffon was waiting on the line, knowing that if he saved this kick Italy would be the World Cup champions. Buffon had made every critical save for the past month. Now, in this final moment, one more save would mean the world for him—literally. The ref blew the whistle, Sagnol approached and shot, Buffon leapt, and the ball went in. Buffon went the wrong way for the fourth straight kick and France was back within one at 4-3.

Now, the scenario was straightforward, a goal from Italy on this kick would win them the World Cup. Because of the red card to Zidane Italy had one extra player to take a penalty. They therefore had to remove one player from the field to put the shootout takers on level terms. Gennaro Gattuso was the player taken out of the mix. There were six choices to take the fifth kick for Italy: Buffon himself (very unlikely), the team captain Cannavaro, the late-game heroics specialist Grosso, the tireless Zambrotta, the least-fatigued Iaquinta, and the best pure goal scorer Luca Toni.

Walking toward the white dot 12 yards from the goal was Fabio Grosso. The man who put Italy into the finals with his goal versus Germany now had a chance to end the final and give Italy their fourth World Cup title. Fabio Grosso and the Italian national team were a mere 12 yards away from destiny. As he prepared to take the kick, Grosso looked skyward, maybe looking for divine intervention, maybe deciding where to place his shot, maybe asking for the spirits of the missed penalty takers of the past to be with him. Donadoni, Serena, Baresi, Massaro, Baggio, Albertini, and Di Biaggio were all standing with Grosso as he took this kick. The referee blew his whistle, possibly for the last time of the entire tournament. Grosso ran to the ball and struck it with his left foot; Barthez dove to his right. The ball flew towards the left into the goal far away from Barthez sending a ripple through the net and sending *Gli Azzuri* into ecstasy.

Italy had won the 2006 FIFA World Cup on a penalty shootout and were world champions for the fourth time.

The players who had been anxiously waiting near midfield all raced towards their teammates for the jubilee. Some ran to chase after Grosso, others leapt into the waiting arms of Buffon. Pirlo couldn't decide where to run so he just sort of drifted aimlessly from near the Buffon pile to near the Grosso pile. The players on the bench, coaches, and trainers all leapt for joy and hugged each other, having reached the goal of every child that has ever kicked a soccer ball. These grown men were running around the field jumping and screaming like children on the last day of school, and the joy was just as innocent and pure. After years of frustration and disappointment, after decades of ghosts and bad dreams, after 24 years without lifting a major trophy, Italy had once again climbed to the top of the world, and they did so in spite of a world rooting against them. The troubles domestically, the scandal, and the future of their league were all totally irrelevant at this moment, the ultimate goal that had been taunting them and haunting them for over 20 years was now accomplished. When Fabio Cannavaro finally lifted the golden trophy into the air, surrounded by his teammates and coaches, his beautiful smile was a sign to the billions of people watching that Italy was once again king of the world. By sacrificing for each other, by continuing to strive in the face of despair, by knowing the precise moments to be at their best, this Italian team had reclaimed their rightful place on the throne of world soccer.

20

Italy 1–France 1
Italy Wins 5-3 on Penalty Kicks

When I saw who the last kicker was going to the penalty spot I honestly thought to myself, "Oh my God, we are going to win the World Cup!" How could Grosso possibly miss? There was no way. After the Australia game and the Germany game he was Italy's golden boy.

There were screams of joy throughout the house. I had always been there to console Mikey. We had sadly embraced after 1998, 2000, and 2002. I instinctively went to grab him, even though this time he wasn't crying. Twenty-four years of disappointment—Poof! Anger and bitterness towards France—Poof! Zidane's legend—Poof! World hunger, war, poverty—Poof! Poof! Poof! It was the happiest moment of my life (you know, except for my wedding day, and the birth of my children, blah, blah, blah).

We all sat glued to the TV, watching the celebration of the players. At this point the three little kids appeared in the room with us. I feel like they weren't there all along, but I really don't remember. Brigid, Alex, and Lorenzo were all wearing their oversized jerseys and sitting in a chair together. Many Italian players sometimes take their shorts off during tournament celebrations and dance around in their underwear. Alex was following their example in just his jersey and diaper. We began the most festive rendition of Funiculì, Funiculà that I had ever heard. Then Mom started chanting "I-TAL-IA" and the three little ones started waving their fingers. Pretty soon we were all yelling and waving our fingers.

I *knew* we were going to win, but I still couldn't believe it. I remember being overly emotional. When the team was finally presented with the trophy and Cannavaro stood on the stand it was something I'll always remember. As he lifted his arms skyward there was an explosion behind him as confetti cannon blasted pieces of paper everywhere. At the exact moment of the cannon shot I felt one tear trickle down my right cheek. I'll never forget that either.

When the television coverage had stopped, we went outside. We took some pictures with all of us and some Italian flags. Then, in the true style of Castellamare we got in our cars and drove around the neighborhood blasting our horns. It wasn't remotely like Italy—not even close—but after 24 years we didn't really care; plus it's the thought that counts.

As I get older I feel as though there aren't a lot of happy moments in adulthood. Adults may be happy, but nothing compares to the happiness that children feel. There is nothing in an adult life that even remotely resembles Christmas morning to an eight-year-old, or seeing Mickey Mouse in person for the first time, or getting a new puppy. I consider myself to be a happy person, but there just aren't thrilling moments for adults like there are for kids. I tell you seriously, I never felt anything at any point in my life as exhilarating as that afternoon celebration.

After a delicious dinner, of which I have no recollection; it was finally time to go home. It seemed like a lifetime ago when I was panicking about the flat tire in Columbus. As I walked to my car I noticed that I had received some messages on my phone, which I turned off before the game. Three people had thought of me and wanted to send me their well wishes. One of them was a recent coworker of mine, John Gardner; the other two were childhood friends, Ray Goodlett and Frank Ponce. It was very nice of those guys to think of me; I still have their messages in my phone to this very day.

When we got back to our house there was just one more piece of business that I had been planning. I went to the trunk of the car and took out the Italian flag that I had taken from my parents' house. I threaded it on a wooden pole that I had also taken from my parents' house. I placed the flag in the flag stand at my front door. It was the first time I had put any flag there; I had been waiting for the right moment. I shut the door, turned out the lights, and went up to bed. I can't think of another night in my life that I slept as well as I did on the night of July 9, 2006.

21

La Vita È Bella
Life Is Beautiful

Italy is the land of many of the most creative minds the world has ever known, so it comes as little surprise that the nation that gave us Dante Aligheiri would have produced a World Cup champion with such a sense of poetry and symbolic retribution. This Italian team erased so many bad memories that the images that made Italians cringe on the morning of July 9, 2006, could be simply laughed off by the morning of July 10, 2006.

In Italia '90, Italy should have lifted the trophy. In that tournament they had an impenetrable defense that didn't allow a goal until the semifinal. They had an incredible goal-scoring sensation called Salvatore Schilacci. "Toto," as he was known, scored game-winning goals in five of Italy's matches on his way to the Golden Boot. Sports are often unfair, so Italy did not win in their homeland, and instead it was Germany who became world champions for the third time, tying Italy as the only other European three-time champion. Now, 16 years later, the Italians have repaid the Germans in full for 1990 and have once again separated themselves from Germany as the only European team to win four World Cup titles.

In 1990, Italy played their semifinal match versus Argentina in Naples, a venue in which the Italian national team had never suffered a defeat. The Germans tried the same scheduling ploy with their semifinal played in Dortmund. Just as Italy was defeated for the first time in Naples, Germany earned their first loss ever in Dortmund. The semifinal in Naples was Italy's first penalty shootout, which they lost to Argentina. Since then, Argentina had never lost a World Cup shootout, until the quarterfinal this year.

In 1994, Italy lost their second consecutive World Cup penalty shootout, this time in the final to Brazil. For Brazil, it was their fourth World Cup championship. This year as Italy claimed their fourth World Cup, they eliminated all the horrible memories of previous shootouts thanks to the final kick from Fabio Grosso. Amazingly, in this shootout, the Italians didn't miss a kick. Another interesting note from the shootout is that neither goalie saved any kicks. The only player not to score was David Trezeguet, who hit the crossbar.

And as for Mr. Trezeguet—the man who scored the game-winning golden goal back in Euro 2000 to steal the victory from Italy and rip out their souls in the process—he ended up in this tournament being the final element in Italy's return to glory. Italy will still shake their heads when thinking about the 2000 European championship, but the anguish of that loss is totally insignificant when compared to the satisfaction of this victory. Dante himself couldn't have created so many ways in which the 2006 World Cup would restore balance and provide a final sense of justice for Italian soccer.

There were many historic trends that were broken by Italy's championship run—the PK shootout streak of defeats, Germany's consecutive victories in Dortmund, the team to score first losing the final, et cetera. But there was one element that did continue a strange historic pattern. Every team has a primary jersey and a secondary one. The primary jersey is the one with which a team is associated—yellow for Brazil, orange for Holland, light blue and white vertical stripes for Argentina, blue for Italy and so on. If two teams with similar primary jerseys meet, one of them has to resort to their alternate colors, and the team that does so always loses: Germany vs. Argentina in the 1986 World Cup final, Argentina vs. Germany in the 1990 final, Italy vs.

France in the 1998 World Cup quarterfinal, Italy vs. France in the European championship in 2000, and finally France vs. Italy in the 2006 World Cup final. It's a good thing that *Gli Azzurri* were able to be so.

The triumph of the Italians was the epitome of sports excellence. The quest took 24 years to accomplish, but it was worth the wait. There was some nostalgia for the Italians of the past two decades who left their mark on *Calcio Italiano* but were unable to share in this team's glory. Paolo Maldini will always be considered one of the best defenders in the history of the game, and he was the image of Italian defense for over a decade, through four World Cups. Christian Vieri was one of the most successful strikers in Italian World Cup history, scoring five goals in 1998, and four more in 2002. Roberto Baggio is one of the greatest players ever, and probably the best Italian to ever wear the national team jersey. He was a young superstar in 1990, as he scored one of the most beautiful goals of that tournament, dribbling through nearly the entire Czechoslovakian defense before the final strike. In 1994, he was the savior for Italy, scoring an equalizer in the final moments against Nigeria to escape an embarrassing defeat, and then leading the team all the way into the finals scoring five goals along the way. Then four years later, as a true veteran leader, he added two more goals before Italy was eliminated in the quarterfinal. These three legends never had the honor to hoist the World Cup trophy, but they were nonetheless instrumental in the success of the current team through their historical significance.

It is ironic that while several of the icons of Italian soccer were unable to reach the ultimate goal of World Cup champion, some previously insignificant players left their indelible mark on this tournament. The Vatican City is the headquarters of the Catholic Church and home of the pope; the city lies within the boundaries of Rome. The Catholics have a large group of holy men and women saints who distinguished themselves through lives of service to God and others. The Holy Father should consider canonizing a new saint,

Fabio Grosso. In order to become a saint, a person needs to perform three miracles. Usually these mystical acts take years to document and verify, but anyone who watched the four weeks of the World Cup can bear witness to Grosso's three miracles: earning the penalty versus Australia, scoring the goal versus Germany, and converting the decisive penalty versus France. There were many bishops and cardinals who watched each Italy match and could easily argue that both the Australia and Germany matches were predestined to go into overtime and a penalty shootout until Grosso's actions. And every Catholic from Sicily to Venice could definitely attest to Italy's inability to win a penalty shootout, so Grosso's final act was also inexplicable by natural means. It seems like Grosso's impending canonization would be a mere formality except for one fact: Pope Benedict XVI is German.

There were other players besides Grosso who will always be remembered for their emergence in this World Cup. Marco Materazzi had been a very capable understudy for his entire career with the national team until this World Cup, where he distinguished himself by making plays on center stage. The goal against Czech Republic held up as the game-winner; the equalizing goal in the final is arguably the most important goal ever scored by Italy in a World Cup. He is clearly no longer the "Vice-Nesta," and although most of the world may remember him as "that guy who Zidane head butted," Italians and true fans of the game will remember him for his essential contributions to Italy's success.

Andrea Pirlo had been a very highly touted player during his days playing for the Italian youth national teams, and although he was a mainstay for the full national team at this point, he had never delivered the virtuoso performances that he did as a youngster. That all changed in Germany 2006. Pirlo was the consistent guiding force for the Italian team. He scored the team's first goal of the tournament and set up several others, including the game-winning goal versus Germany and the equalizer against France. He was a hardworking midfielder who also possessed incredible skills with the ball. He rarely used any flashy moves, but everything he did contained a quiet confidence that made his teammates better.

Simone Perrotta, Mauro Camoranesi, and Gennaro Gattuso did not score a goal in the World Cup. It seemed like they were the only players on the team who didn't score, but Italians know that even though it can go undetected at times, the roles filled by these players are critical. There is no way that Pirlo and Totti could have had the freedom to move forward into the attack without the defensive balance of these players. They each play with remarkable fortitude and determination (Perrotta played the final 20 or so minutes of the U.S.A. match with a painful leg injury since Lippi had used all of his substitutions). The hard-nosed play of these players added an additional element of strength and toughness to an already rock-solid group. These players normally don't make their way into the spotlight, but during the celebration of the final victory, Camoranesi did. His trademark long ponytail had been bouncing around throughout the tournament, and he had told his teammates that he wouldn't cut his hair until he won the championship. Before officially accepting the trophy at the medal stand, the team brought a chair onto the field, made a circle around him and actually cut his hair right on the field.

The Italian defense was the one aspect of the team that was expected to succeed. The Italians have always taken a great deal of pride in defending, but even the typically airtight defense was more suffocating than usual. Cannavaro, Buffon, Zambrotta, Grosso, Materazzi, Nesta, Zaccardo and Barzagli all contributed to establish one of the most formidable defenses ever in the World Cup. Italy became the only World Cup champion to go an entire tournament without allowing the opponent to score in the run of play. The two goals scored against Italy were an own goal and a penalty kick. It is hard to imagine another team ever duplicating this feat. Team captain Fabio Cannavaro earned the Silver Ball by receiving the second most votes for tournament most valuable player. He lost out to Zidane, probably because the media voting took place before Zidane's head butt. There is no doubt which player would like to trade trophies and which one would not. Galileo once said, "Mathematics is the language with which God has written the Universe." As proof of this theory, look no farther than Cannavaro. The World Cup final was his 100th career match played with the Italian national team. Certainly the stars were aligned for Cannavaro and his teammates, and now the stars will be aligned on the Italian uniforms—four stars.

The Italians have always been well known for staunch defending, but in this tournament the varied attack may have been even better than the defense. Marcello Lippi included six strikers on his 23-man roster, an unusually high number for a team famous for defense. It is also odd to bring along so many forwards since so few get to play at a time, but for Lippi the thought process proved to be an excellent one. All six of the strikers, Toni, Gilardino, Totti, Del Piero, Iaquinta, and Inzaghi scored. The balance was perfect, and the efficiency was even better, especially for Filippo Inzaghi, who managed to score a goal despite playing only 30 minutes in his lone appearance of the World Cup.

Daniele De Rossi had a good opening match versus Ghana, but it was quickly forgotten after his brutal foul and red card in match number two versus U.S.A. He was fortunate that his teammates made their way to the final without him. De Rossi should be even more grateful to his coach for having the faith in him to actually put him in the game after his long absence. De Rossi did help clog up the French attack for the 50 minutes that he was on the field, and then he made his most important contribution by converting his penalty in the shootout.

There were also a handful of players who were unable to make a real impact on the field: the backup goalkeepers Angelo Peruzzi and Marco Amelia never got to set foot on the field in Germany, while Simone Barone and Massimo Oddo each played less than 50 total minutes throughout the tournament. Nobody should feel sorry for them though, as there are millions of professional players all over the world who would trade anything to win the World Cup. Plus, in all of the training and preparation before and during the World Cup every player is needed to maintain the proper work ethic and mentality throughout the team.

On Monday afternoon, the day after the World Cup victory, the Italian team returned home and was greeted by thousands of fans that had flocked to the airport to meet their heroes. This team had taken the entire nation on an unforgettable journey over the past month. The tournament began with such doubts on so many levels, but the perseverance of this group of men was far more powerful than any of the negative factors that would have surely derailed a team with less determination and strength. The Italian people once again had a clear reason to be proud of Italian soccer. The greed, deceit, and corruption of the top Italian league were totally overshadowed by the pride, solidarity, and success of the national team. When the Italians went to Germany they left all of the problems they had back in Italy, and managed to play the best soccer of their lives. They were able to approach the tournament as a showcase of the game they had loved all their lives and distanced themselves from the politics and business aspects that sometimes make even the most devoted player forget why he started playing in the first place.

For thousands of years, Italian masters have created marvelous works of art that stand the test of time by continuing to be amazing things of beauty to this day. From the Colosseum to St. Peter's Cathedral, from *La Scala* Opera House to the University of Bologna, there are countless examples of the way that Italians throughout time have been masters of creation. The Renaissance in Italy produced many of the great masters, but now there is another famous Italian whose masterpiece has changed Italy for the better once again.

As Italy was beginning their final preparation for the tournament, there were those who thought Marcello Lippi should be replaced due to his connection with the corruption of Serie A. Lippi refused to resign. Throughout the tournament, Lippi made tactical changes and adjustments, all of which worked out perfectly. His knowledge of the game was never questioned, but it was not strategy or positioning that made his job a success. Somehow Lippi managed to have his team totally focused for every moment of play. There were bad stretches for the Italians and many mistakes made on the field, but there was never a moment of any game when the team was not putting forth maximum effort. The team was ideally prepared for everything that might come their way, and although the players deserve the credit for making the right plays when necessary, the coach can take pride in being the individual who put the players in the right places to succeed. Lippi showed extreme respect and trust for his players, and these sentiments were reciprocated, illustrated by the various times that players ran to the bench to celebrate goals with the coach. A few days after the final match, Lippi announced his resignation as national team coach. The decision was not a shocking one, but it was disappointing to see the end of an era so soon after it began. Marcello Lippi was truly the mastermind behind the success of the Italian national team, and his expert guidance that led Italy to the World Cup championship will ensure that his name is as cemented in Italian history as the likes of Michelangelo and Leonardo.

This specific group of 23 players will never be assembled together again. In future matches and tournaments there will be slight modifications that may produce similar results, but cannot equal the uniqueness of this group. It is impossible to measure the profound impact that this World Cup champion team will have on the Italian people. The images of Germany 2006 will live on for generations throughout Italy and also for all Italians worldwide. Italian fans will always remember Fabio Cannavaro standing on the podium lifting the World Cup trophy high into the air as confetti fell from the sky all around him and his teammates. Years from now grandparents will tell stories to their grandchildren about how Fabio Grosso made sure that Italy never lost a World Cup game to Germany. Young goalkeepers will always try to emulate the greatness of Gigi Buffon, and any spectacular saves made by Italian goalies in the future will undoubtedly be compared to Buffon's magnificent stop in extra time against Zidane.

This Italian team changed the lives of all the individuals who supported them during this march to greatness. No matter what happens to Italian soccer over the course of the next 100 years, this team can never be replaced. They will always be remembered for displaying the true beauty of the game, playing so selflessly for each other. For the true fans of *Gli Azzurri*, this experience will always be the highlight of sports excellence. Italians around the globe owe a debt of gratitude that can never be repaid to this group of extraordinary men who in a remarkable span of 31 days altered the lives of millions forever.

22

The New World

When I woke up on Monday, July 10, my life was more or less the same, except that everything was totally different. Meg went to work, I stayed home with Lorenzo, and it was just like the start of a regular work week. There was one difference. Everybody knows what it feels like when you wake up to start another work week—the way you feel when the alarm goes off on a Monday morning. That feeling was absent for me on Monday, July 10; for me it felt like it was Thursday afternoon of a four-day weekend. I would feel that way for many days to come.

Looking back I feel as though I went a little overboard in my celebrations. First, I bought every item of Italy championship apparel that I could find, unless it was totally hideous. As soon as I saw an item in a soccer catalogue I bought it. Fortunately, there were very few articles that were not totally hideous, so I really only ended up buying a few shirts. One was a T-shirt that was designed like the Italy jersey. On the front was the phrase "campioni del mondo," world champions, with the number 4 surrounded by four stars. Every time a nation wins the World Cup, the team earns a star to be worn on their jersey. Now, Italy had become only the second team ever to earn four stars, behind the five stars of Brazil. All around the top of the shirt were the autographs of the 23 players and head coach, all signed in gold. This same shirt was also designed as a replica jersey, but I went for the less expensive, more comfortable T-shirt. Besides being a fashionable addition to my wardrobe, the shirt was also a mystery game. To win the game you had to decipher which chicken-scratch signature belonged to which player.

If you know anybody who went to elementary school in Italy, then you know that they have the worst handwriting possible. I studied Italian in college, and whether my professors wrote in English or Italian, I had no idea what the message was. The letters are nothing like the way Arabic letters are used in other parts of the world. There is no way to decipher between a lower-case G and the number 9, the letter P always looks like 1 degree Fahrenheit, and the number 4 is impossible to distinguish from a lightning bolt. I once had an assignment in college on which I received a four out of four (4/4); I thought Shazam had autographed my homework.

So, at the top of the shirt there are 24 scribbles that make for hours of fun while trying to decipher. It took me about 20 minutes to actually identify the 24 different signatures, since it's hard to tell when one stops and the next begins. From that point there were about ten players who wrote their numbers next to their name, but amazingly enough that didn't help very much. One player's name was simple to read, and he also wrote his number. S. Barone, #17. Perfect. My suspicion is that he wrote his name so clearly to make sure that nobody would ever forget that he was on the team. He didn't make a major impact on the field, and even though I'll always remember him as the guy who would have scored if Inzaghi had shared, I don't blame his careful penmanship. Alberto Gilardino's last name was hard to read, but Alberto was fairly clear, so since the team didn't have an Alberto J. Inntimo, which is what it looked like, his name was soon identified. There were five other players whose names were illegible, but their numbers were clear enough. Then there were two other numbers that could be assumed: £2 stands for 22, and ^5 for 15. From that point it got pretty difficult. Through a careful process of elimination, we (my family helped) were finally able to definitively identify 22 of the 24 names. The last two names will always remain a mystery, since Luca

Toni and Francesco Totti have such similar last names and neither dots their i's.

Mikey then spearheaded an initiative for each of us to buy a replica jersey of our favorite players. Through the modern marvel of eBay, he found a new Andrea Pirlo jersey for a very good price. He told us that there were a bunch of shirts for cheap, and he didn't have to tell us twice. We each purchased the jersey of a different player: Pep got Fabio Cannavaro, I got Luca Toni, Nori got Alessandro Del Piero (her longtime "boyfriend"), Johnny got Fabio Grosso, and Gio got Gianluca Zambrotta. I tried to convince Meg to buy a shirt, but she thought that one such shirt was more than enough for our house. Mikey disagreed as he purchased an additional Alberto Gilardino and Gennaro Gattuso shirt for himself. Now, Mikey can dress according to his mood. If he's feeling like a calm leader he'll wear the Pirlo shirt, but if he feels feisty and ready to start a fight he'll put on Gattuso's #8.

I bought one more T-shirt, a blue one with the phrase "La Quarta Stella," meaning the fourth star. The shirt had four stars upon which were written the years of the four times Italy won the World Cup: '34, '38, '82, and '06. I wore this shirt to a D.C. United practice when I was doing an interview. Ben Olsen, who I was not interviewing, came up to me and said something to the extent of, "Come on, man. You can't really count 1934 and 1938!" I responded, "Why? Do you think Mussolini had something to do with it?" He said, "All I know is there was a lot of funny stuff going on back then." I don't think he was mad at me, maybe he just thought that his team should've beaten mine in Germany.

The player I had gone to interview was Freddy Adu. Freddy was a media darling since he entered MLS at age 14, but I never treated him differently than Jaime Moreno or Ben Olsen. I do think that by the time Freddy retires, he will be without a doubt the greatest American soccer player ever. It was Freddy's third year with the team, so we had talked many times, and he knew that I was an Italy fan. As he was walking over to talk to me he was wearing his beaming smile, and he said, "Hey, Italy! Congratulations!" He was the only member of D.C. United (player, coach, or staff member) who actually congratulated me on Italy's win. Freddy Adu, who was easily the biggest star in terms of celebrity status, was the only person who expressed that he was at least in some ways happy for me. Freddy is not your typical superstar.

Time went on, and little by little, the thrill of the Italy victory started to wear off just a little bit. After a couple of weeks, everyone came over to our house for dinner. As Pop was leaving he asked me, "How long are you going to keep that flag up?" indicating the Italian flag at my front door. I thought, "Um, you know, for the next four years." I told him, "Not much longer." I took it down the next day.

There have been many fringe benefits from my job with D.C. United, the best of which was that I received a championship ring when they won the league crown in 2004. The next best bonus was one that I received in August of 2006. D.C. United was going to Seattle, Washington, to play an international friendly match against Real Madrid. In case you don't know, Real Madrid is the most storied team in Spain, and one of the greatest clubs in the history of soccer. I was going to Seattle to call the radio play-by-play. Real Madrid was also the new team of Fabio Cannavaro, who left Juventus in the midst of their relegation to the Italian second division. About 90 minutes prior to kickoff, I made my way down to the locker room to conduct an interview with D.C.'s head coach Peter Nowak. Usually, the teams arrive at the stadium about an hour and a half before game time. As I was waiting for the United bus, the Real Madrid bus rolled in and dropped off some of the greatest players in the world, an amazing collection of World Cup stars: Robinho and Roberto Carlos of Brazil, David Beckham of England, Ruud Van Nistelrooy of Holland, Iker Casillas of Spain, and the list goes on and on. Near the end of the group were two players that I had been looking for, Cannavaro and Antonio Cassano. Cassano was another Italian national team player who had not been selected to play on the World Cup roster. He had a reputation as sort of a troublemaker, but I always liked the way he played and thought he got a little bit of a bad rap. As the two Italians walked towards me on their way into the locker room I said to them in Italian, "Hey guys, good evening." They politely responded, "Good evening," maybe a little surprised that someone spoke their native language. They were walking past me, and I knew I should say something else to Cannavaro. I planned on shaking his hand, but he was moving quicker than I thought, so I ended up sort of grabbing his arm. He looked back at me and I said in Italian, "Congratulations, and thank you." He didn't say anything, but he had a huge smile on his face. It was the same smile he had worn when he lifted the trophy in Berlin exactly one month earlier. His smile was absolutely radiant, and without words his smile said, "You're welcome." Cannavaro was the most beautiful man I had ever seen. I don't know if he would remember our brief conversation, but when he looked me in the eye with that smile on his face, I got the feeling that he was happy to meet one of the millions of people across the world whose life he had changed for the better. In front of 66,830 spectators and an electric atmosphere, D.C. United tied Real Madrid 1-1.

The remembrances kept on coming throughout the year. Nori had gone to Italy in August, and returned with little jerseys for Brigid, Alex, and Lorenzo. She also brought an Italy team photo with the words "Campioni Del Mondo" for each of her brothers (I think they were being handed out for free whenever people landed at an Italian airport). For my 30th birthday in October, Meg got me a four-pack Italy World Cup Champions DVD collection made by the Italian media. The series is incredible and quickly became the best DVD gift that Meg ever gave me, surpassing the film *Maverick*. My in-laws gave me two framed glossy copies of *The Washington Post* from the day after the World Cup: the front page and the front page of the Sports section. They hang near my TV in the basement, right below the team picture that Nori gave me. All of the wonderful gifts and mementos I acquired in the wake of Italy's championship are all very special to me, but they are just material reminders of the true gift given to me by that group of Italians during the magical summer of 2006.

I don't know if Italy will win another World Cup in my lifetime, or if they ever will. As a true fan I am very grateful to have had the opportunity to wholeheartedly support a team that won the World Cup. Many fans who love their teams as much as I love Italy may never get to see their team hoist the world's most precious trophy. I certainly hope Italy wins another World Cup—I hope they win in 2010—but to focus on winning the next one is selfish and irresponsible. No matter how good a team is, winning the World Cup is incredibly difficult. If a player, coach, or fan is fortunate enough to be a part of a World Cup champion, then they should cherish every moment of it, and not waste an instant thinking about the future. At most, you can only celebrate winning the World Cup for four years, and since this experience has been so incredible for me I will ride the wave of emotions as far as it takes me.

No matter what happens over the course of the next 20 World Cups, I will always have Germany 2006. If Italy never wins another World Cup match, I will always think fondly of Vincenzo Iaquinta's goal versus Ghana and the ensuing celebration, the moment in which the referee pointed to the penalty spot against Australia, Fabio Grosso's miraculous goal versus Germany, and Fabio Cannavaro standing on top of the championship podium. These are moments that I will remember as long as my memory continues to function, and I can never repay the people responsible for the overwhelming joy that they unknowingly enabled me to have. Fabio Grosso scoring the final penalty kick of the shootout was a moment that changed my life and changed the world. After all, the entire world looked happily on the image of the Italian celebration since it signaled the unofficial beginning of the 2010 World Cup.

23

June 9, 2007

It is our sixth wedding anniversary. Lorenzo is getting bigger and smarter every day. The 2006 FIFA World Cup began one year ago today, and I still remember many details like they happened yesterday. It was one year ago today that Paulo Wanchope scored in the 12th minute of the opening match versus Germany to tie the score. The goal was a shock to the home nation and to most of the world. Only the people from the CONCACAF region knew about how good the Costa Rican striker was. It only took the Germans five minutes to pull in front again, this time for good, but I still remember the excitement of Costa Rica being temporarily even with the powerful Germans. The opening match finished 4-2 for Germany, but my favorite memory of Opening Day 2006 was Wanchope's equalizer.

Earlier this week, Team Italy won two matches to improve their position in qualifying for Euro 2008. There was a little bit of World Cup hangover for the Italians as they began qualifying for the European championship. In their first match after becoming world champions they tied at home to Lithuania, ouch. Then in a World Cup final rematch they were defeated 3-1 in France in front of a raucous crowd. I was upset that Italy lost, but certainly there was a little bit of solace from the match two months earlier. Italy righted the ship after the two bad games and has a good chance to qualify for Euro 2008.

The new Italian head coach is a former player named Roberto Donadoni. He was a really good player for the national team for about ten years. Near the end of his career he actually came to the United States to play in MLS with the New York/New Jersey MetroStars as the franchise was known in 1996. As a D.C. United fan/employee I was a little skeptical when Team Italy hired a former MetroStar (they are D.C.'s biggest rival), but if the people who hired Lippi think that his successor should be Donadoni, who am I to argue?

There was an article I saw a few weeks ago about a baby boom in Italy. I think the article referred to the rise in Italian pregnancies as "Championship Babies." I bet there will be a lot of baby boys in Italy named Fabio in the next year or so. Right around the turn of the New Year, Meg and I learned that we were expecting a new baby ourselves. We had the ultrasound a few months later and found out that Lorenzo was going to have a little brother. As promised, we'll name him Luca. I'm still pushing Fabio as a middle name. Pep and Kristen are also expecting a son who will be only a few weeks younger than Luca. Since Kristen has always had a crush on Mr. Buffon, I might have a new nephew named Gianluigi.

Just like last summer, Anna and Laura are coming to stay with my parents, study English, practice ballet, and tan at the pool. In the midst of the D.C. United season, South America is holding their continental championship known as Copa America. I was talking with Christian Gomez about it recently, and he was really excited since Argentina was bringing in all of their superstars. I'd be happy to support Christian and Facundo in their nation's quest for the title were it not for one thing. Team U.S.A. was a guest participant in the tournament, and somehow Ben Olsen is back on the team. I have too many international friends.

The initial power of Italy's victory from a year ago has certainly diminished over time, but not as much as I thought. I truly think that every single day since the final match I have thought about the Italy team at least once. Whenever Italy lost a significant tournament I would think about it all the time. Many times on the night of a sad defeat I would actually dream that Italy had won, only to wake up realizing the truth and reliving the defeat again. I considered it a major step in the grieving process when I could go an entire day without thinking about the loss. For the worst losses it usually took about two or three months. Now, since I'm still celebrating, I'm glad to not go a whole day without remembering. I'm pleased to say that I've been celebrating Italy's triumph for much longer than I ever mourned even their most upsetting defeat. That's the way it should be.

My family has plans to go to Italy in the summer of 2008. The final plans will depend on the D.C. United schedule, but I haven't been to Italy since 2000, and I feel like it's the right time to have Lorenzo and Luca meet their cousins in Castellamare. If everything goes according to plan, we should be able to watch Italy play in the Euro Cup while with my cousins. It will be nice to share more Italian soccer with them like I did when I was younger. Looking back it would have been great to experience the Italy World Cup championship in person with my Italian relatives, but in all honesty I can't say that I would change anything at all from the 2006 FIFA World Cup.

Printed in the United Kingdom
by Lightning Source UK Ltd.
135006UK00001B/106/P

9 781604 746075